Welcome to
Photoshop
5 Minute Tips & Fixes

Photoshop is an amazing piece of software that lets us do
practically anything with our digital photos. It's easy to get
lost for hours, playing around with the tools, tweaking and creating
masterpieces. Sometimes, however, you just want to open the program,
make the change you need and be finished in minutes.

That's exactly what this book is for: making quick fixes and adding creative
effects to your photos. Every project in this book can be completed in just
five minutes, and there are in-depth guides to Photoshop's essential tools
so that you can get more comfortable with using them in a flash. We also
look at how you can use automated options to speed up your workflow,
as well as customise Photoshop to work exactly as you need it.

With over 160 pages of tips, tricks and fixes, it's the ultimate timesaving
guide to Photoshop and Photoshop Elements.

Enjoy the book.

Imagine Publishing Ltd
Richmond House
33 Richmond Hill
Bournemouth
Dorset BH2 6EZ
☎ +44 (0) 1202 586200
Website: www.imagine-publishing.co.uk

Editor in Chief
Jo Cole

Editor
Julie Bassett

Design
Danielle Dixon

Printed by
William Gibbons, 26 Planetary Road, Willenhall, West Midlands, WV13 3XT

Distributed in the UK & Eire by
Imagine Publishing Ltd, www.imagineshop.co.uk. Tel 01202 586200

Distributed in Australia by
Gordon & Gotch, Equinox Centre, 18 Rodborough Road, Frenchs Forest,
NCW 2000. Tel + 01 2 9972 8800

Distributed in the Rest of the World by
Marketforce, Blue Fin Building, 110 Southwark Street, London, SE1 0SU

Disclaimer

IMAGINE
PUBLISHING

Contents

08
5 minute fixes
Get started with this collection of quick-fix tips and tricks

After
Before

88

Basic corrections

Get creative

Icons explained:

Add depth using textures

Create super-fast sketch effects

Quick fix: Speedy tricks to transform photos in seconds

Tool tricks: In-depth guides to Photoshop's key tools

Before

After

119

92

After
Before

100

42

Use a gradient map for a splash of colour

Work faster

Troubleshooting

Sharpen detail

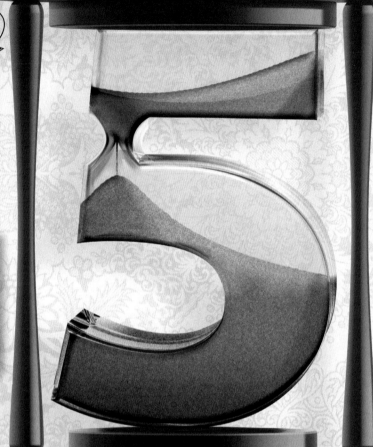

Photo effects

minute fixes

We round up some of the best edits that you can use to improve your images in a mere five minutes (or less!)

While there is a lot to be said for settling down to a mammoth Photoshop session where you tinker and tweak an image into pristine glory, there are times when you just want a quick solution. A lot of common problems can be sorted out in minutes.

Over the next few pages, we are going to be sharing some of the techniques we use when time, patience or concentration is in short supply. We'll be fixing obvious problems such as dull colour or soft edges in addition to looking at creative solutions for pepping up an image. Sometimes a photo will only ever be okay no

matter how bright its colours or how in focus it is. However, by giving it a sketch effect, for example, you can create an entirely different image that has the ability to really stand out.

We even have a couple of suggestions for improving your Photoshop workflow, giving you extra time for more creative projects!

Spring into action

Save time by teaching Photoshop to do repetitive tasks for you

Do you find that you end up performing the same tasks time and time again without ever changing any settings? Perhaps something like Auto-tone, Sharpen More and adding a vignette through the Filter>Lens Correction feature. Or maybe there's a particular type of framing, watermark or signature you like to add to all your photography. Possibly you are tasked with rotating and cropping 300 scanned photos and you can feel your soul being crushed beneath the monotony.

Regardless of what it is, if it's so repetitive you feel like you could train a monkey to do it, then let us be the ones to tell you that Photoshop is smarter than that monkey! Instead of you being the one performing the tasks, define custom actions that can be triggered at a single keystroke and shave precious minutes off your production time. This allows you to focus your creative attention on your design work instead of getting tied up with repetitive button pushing.

01 Is this thing on? Open the Actions palette (Opt/Alt+F9) and select a folder to place your action in or create a new one using the 'Create a new set' icon at the bottom. Press the 'Create new action' icon also found in the footer of the palette. Give the action a name for easily referring back to it later, and then press the Record button.

02 One step at a time Carefully go through each step of your process. You don't need to be quick, but you do need to be accurate. Photoshop isn't recording time, just menu selections and tool usage. You can watch the steps build up in the Actions palette. When you are finished, press the Stop button in the footer to halt the recording.

03 At the press of a button... Now you can test out the action you have created by hitting the Play button and watching it work. Double-click to the right of the action's name to get the Action Options box again. Assign a function key using the drop-down menu, and now the entire action can be run at the press of a single button.

Correct colour casts

Pull a natural hue out of a poorly coloured pic

Get your hues as they should be by fixing colour casts

We may not notice the difference between the light generated by a fluorescent bulb and a halogen one, but photographs taken with different light sources will show great differences in colour. This is compensated for by setting the white balance on the camera, or letting a sensor automatically do that for you. Colour casts are usually the result of a photograph taken with an inaccurate white balance setting. This generates an image with a distinct tint due to the error. The way to correct this is to remap the white, grey or black points, as this allows the colours to settle back into the more expected values. Follow the steps below to easily remove all but the most drastic of colour casts and get the tones just right.

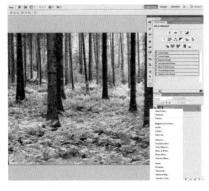

01 Adjustments are required Begin by adding a Curves adjustment layer. Look for the small icon in the foot of the Layers palette that looks like a circle that is half black and half white. Clicking on that icon activates a list of available adjustment layers, then simply select the Curves option from there.

02 Black and white points In the Adjustments palette to the left of the histogram window you will see three small eyedropper icons. Begin by clicking the black eyedropper and sampling a portion of your image that should be completely black. Likewise, use the white eyedropper in the same way to sample the brightest pixels to set the white point.

03 Kill the colour cast Using the grey eyedropper is the most effective and most difficult step in the process. The goal is to use it to sample a pixel that should be 50% grey. This may take several attempts before getting a good setting. If the first click yields poor results, simply try another area of pixels. Taking the time for a little trial and error is well worth it here.

Don't let a grey sky ruin your day – use gradients to fix it

Photo edit

Better, brighter skies

Chase away those grey days with this easy sky repair

Top tip: Gradients are also useful for improving dull sunset images – pick reds or oranges for the best effect.

01 Select-a-sky Begin by using the Quick Selection tool to select your sky area. If the tool grabs areas of the image you don't want, hold down the Opt/Alt key and paint over the area to remove from the selection. Depending on your version, the selection can be edited further by using the Refine Edge button if this is needed.

02 New masked layer Press the 'Add new layer' button in the foot of the Layers palette. The selection is automatically converted into a mask. This will limit the effect to the sky, and having it on a new layer protects your original Background layer from any direct alteration. Set this layer's blending mode to Overlay.

03 Fade away the grey Set your Foreground colour to a nice, bright sky blue. Grab the Gradient tool and use the Foreground to Transparent preset in the Options bar. Make sure the mode is set to Linear, click at the top of your canvas and drag straight down towards the horizon (or your foreground object) to create a blue gradient that fades away.

Photo edit

Boost colours and sharpness

Transform a shot from dull and blurry to bright and crisp

Colour and detail: two elements that can make or break any photo. If one is missing, the other one better be something special to compensate. If both are weak, you know you are in trouble. But all is not lost! This neat little trick can do wonders for a shot that is a little too dull as well as being a bit soft. It can infuse the image with life and give it a pop that demands attention. That being said, it cannot perform miracles. If the photo is devoid of colour and detail, this won't help. There has to be something there to work with. If that is the case with your image, we encourage you to try this technique out.

Make an image pop by turning attention to the colour

01 Pull out the details Create a copy of the Background layer to work with. Go to Filter>Sharpen>Unsharp Mask and work with the settings until you can see some details from the image being revealed. In this example we used an Amount of 72%, Radius of 4.8 pixels and Threshold of 5 levels. Your results may vary depending on the image.

02 Add Vibrance Add a Vibrance adjustment layer by clicking the Vibrance icon in the Adjustments palette. Pump up the Vibrance slider, then increase the saturation. Beware of blowing out the colour tones. If needed, use the layer mask that's automatically added to paint out the adjustment where it is not required.

03 Final pop Now create a composite layer on the top of the stack by pressing Cmd/Ctrl+Alt+Shift+E, and then on this new layer go to Filter>Other>High Pass. Enter a setting of 3 pixels and press OK. Change the layer's blending mode to Overlay to give a final touch of edge sharpening, and your image should be infinitely improved.

GPU settings

Get the most out of those advanced features by using GPU

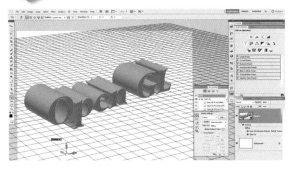

You may have heard other users rave about some of the slick new features found in Photoshop CS5, only to be confused as to why you can't seem to find them. We're talking about features such as the Rotate View tool, Scrubby Zoom, the ability to resize your brush right on the canvas or even that mysterious Repousse tool. All could be hidden from your experience. Perhaps you've even checked to make sure you have a graphics card capable of heavy lifting, yet you still seem to be missing out on the joy of these new features. The most likely reason for your deflated performance is because you don't have your GPU or Graphics Processing Unit set up correctly. All of these features and more rely on something called OpenGL drawing, and they won't appear without it. Once you do turn it on, it can transform your Photoshop experience in minutes, so read on and we'll show you what you need to do.

01 Performance preferences Go to Edit> Preferences>Performance and look for the GPU Settings box. It will list your graphics card and you should see a checkbox for Enable OpenGL Drawing. Place a check in that box and then hit the Advanced Settings box. Select a mode of your choice. We recommend Normal.

02 Give it a whirl You will need to close down any documents you have open in Photoshop and then open them again to take advantage of the newly enabled OpenGL settings. To test if things are working, hold down the R key and then drag your mouse in a circle. The canvas should spin around as you move your cursor.

03 Repousse fun Just to see the true power of the advanced CS5 extended features and OpenGL, try this. Put down some text on your canvas. Make it something big and bold in a large, fat font. Then go to 3D>Repousse>Text Layer to have Photoshop transform your text into a real, honest to goodness 3D object!

Remove unwanted elements

Clean up photos with the Clone Stamp tool

This is the tool that Photoshop is arguably the best known for. It is the technique that tabloids use to remove people from one picture and deftly place them into another. While we don't condone the practice of personal slander on a celebrity, we fully embrace the idea of altering a photo to create a better shot aesthetically. In this example, we begin with a peaceful and serene beach shot that would be even more peaceful and serene if it didn't contain the handful of people on the shore line and a tacky, fruit-themed bus cluttering up the horizon. The process for cloning out items is pretty straightforward, but we will say that it does take a practised eye to do it well. The trick is learning where to best set the source point to avoid obvious repetition or paint strokes, but even those can be cleaned up afterwards.

Create your perfect vista using the Clone Stamp tool

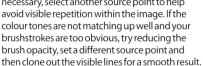

01 Clone Stamp setup Begin by creating a copy of the Background layer to work with, then grab the Clone Stamp tool and set the brush tip to a soft round brush. Find an area that looks similar in content and colour value to the area you wish to clone out, then hold down the Opt/Alt key and click once to set the source point for your cloning.

02 Selective source When selecting a source point, use an area that's easy to match. For example, setting our source point to the horizon makes alignment simple for the new painted area. After setting the source point, Photoshop gives you a helpful overlay on the brush so you can see what pixels you are about to lay down on the image before you commit.

03 Clone away Use short, gentle strokes to remove the unwanted element. If necessary, select another source point to help avoid visible repetition within the image. If the colour tones are not matching up well and your brushstrokes are too obvious, try reducing the brush opacity, set a different source point and then clone out the visible lines for a smooth result.

Easy aged photo effect

Age a photo 50 years in five minutes

Aged photos have their own special charm and personality. The condition of the photo itself tells a story with the way it fades and cracks with time. It makes you wonder if the story of the photo paper is more interesting than the story of the photograph. We'll show you how to easily capture that effect quickly and painlessly. This technique makes use of adjustment layers, smart filters and layer styles, so, even though the whole idea is to destroy the photo, this effect is really non-destructive. Grab a photo you want to push back in time and follow along with these steps.

Travel back in time by giving your image an aged look

Top tip: If you have a photo that you love but that suffers from awkward colour or tonal problems, save yourself editing time by transforming it into an aged image.

01 Smart Object Right-click on the Background layer in the Layers palette and select Convert to Smart Object. Next, create a rectangular selection just inside the frame and press the 'Add layer mask' icon (the white circle in a grey box). Add a new layer beneath the photo and fill it with an off-white shade to begin altering the tones of your image.

02 Black and white Add a Channel Mixer adjustment layer above the photograph original. Tick the Monochrome box and adjust the sliders to give a high contrast effect. You want blown out highlights and strong shadows to make the photo look faded.

03 Gradient Map Next, add a Gradient Map adjustment layer and choose the Black, White setting from the list of presets. Click on the gradient to open the Gradient Editor and change the black stopper on the left to a coppery-brown tone. We used '#6a5342'. This gives the photo a sepia, aged colour.

04 Smart filters Go to the photo Smart Object and add a Gaussian Blur (Filter>Blur>Gaussian Blur) of 4 pixels. Then go to Filter>Noise>Add Noise and set the Amount to 14%, Distribution to Gaussian and check the Monochromatic box. This makes sure the photo doesn't have that sleek, modern crispness to it.

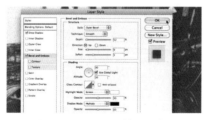

05 Layer styles Next add a new layer to the top of the stack and assign the following layer styles: Drop Shadow with Opacity at 45%, Distance at 12, Spread at 0 and Size at 29; Bevel and Emboss with Style set to Outer Bevel, Depth set to 52%, Size at 9 pixels, Soften at 5 pixels and Highlight/Shadow at 50%.

06 Painted cracks Grab a small irregular paint brush. We used the Chalk 11 tip with the size reduced to around 6 pixels. Set the paint colour to a light grey and carefully draw some cracks and folds at random points on the photo. The layer style will appear as you paint. Finish by setting the blend mode to Screen, reduce the Opacity to 39% and you're done.

Rich sepia tones

This sepia trick allows for maximum control

01 Level up Begin by adding a Levels adjustment layer. In the Histogram palette, pull the outer slider handles in to meet the edges of the histogram chart. This should increase the overall contrast of the image. Take the midpoint slider and move it slightly to the left to brighten the image a bit so that it will work when desaturated.

02 Black and white Next add a Black and White adjustment layer over the Levels adjustment. In the Adjustments palette, look for the drop-down menu near the top. These are presets used to create different flavours of black and white effects. Here we used the Neutral Density settings for our image of the running horses.

03 Photo Filter Finally, add a Photo Filter adjustment layer. From the filter drop-down, select the Sepia option. If the colourisation isn't strong enough to suit you, increase the Density slider to enhance the effect. Try the Preserve Luminosity checkmark both on and off to see which setting works best for your image.

Fake focal blur

Use a manufactured focal blur to make your subjects stand out

There's nothing quite like putting focus on a subject by actually putting focus on that subject. Or more accurately, removing focus from the areas around the subject. Most photographs already have a focal blur built into them. It's what the term 'in focus' means; that the primary subject of the photo is in the focal setting of the camera's lens. Different lenses have different focal lengths creating different effects or focal blurs and one way to enhance the focus of a photo's subject is to manufacture focal blur around it. This technique shows a precise method for doing just that. A frequently overlooked feature of Photoshop is the Lens Blur feature, which not only does an outstanding job of simulating actual focal blurs, but can even be set to read a depth map that's been saved to a channel. This allows Photoshop to calculate a more accurate effect.

Draw attention to your subjects with some deft blur

01 Isolate the subject Begin by creating a copy of the Background layer to work on, then form a selection around the subject using the selection tool of your choice. In this statue image we used the Pen tool because of its supreme accuracy. Once the selection is done, press Cmd/Ctrl+J to copy the subject to its own layer, then turn of its visibility.

02 Remove the subject On the background copy layer, use the Content Aware Fill feature or the Clone Stamp tool to roughly remove the subject. Then press 'Q' to enter Quick Mask mode and use the Gradient tool to drag a white to black linear gradient down from the horizon line to the subject. Press 'Q' again and save the selection (Select>Save Selection).

03 Lens Blur Go to Filter>Blur>Lens Blur. In the area labelled Depth Map, set the Source to the selection you saved in the previous step. If the blur effect appears backwards, check the Invert box. Adjust the settings to get a blur suitable for your image and press OK. Then turn the visibility of the subject layer back on.

Photoshop's sketchbook

Turn a photo into a digital sketch

Make art from your photos with this useful technique

This technique is ideal for quickly simulating a lovely, hand-sketched effect. There are other, more complicated techniques out there you could employ that involve a lot more than just a few minutes' worth of filter wrangling, and ultimately we fully encourage you to develop your own hand skills so you can create a true sketch by hand. There's no tricks or tips that can ever replace that. But when it comes to quick, clean and effective, when you need a filter-based sketch effect that is easy and convincing, this tip is hard to beat!

Top tip: To make the effect even more realistic, get an image of a sketchbook and copy and paste your picture into it with the Multiply blending mode to make it sit on the page.

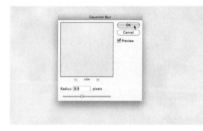

01 Set the sketchbook Begin by creating a new layer for the sketch paper. Set your Foreground and Background colours to light parchment hues that are slightly different from each other. Go to Filter>Render>Clouds to fill the layer and then go to Filter>Blur>Gaussian Blur and blur the pattern until the colours bleed into each other and look natural.

02 Black and white effect Duplicate the Background layer and move the copy above the parchment layer. Go to Image>Adjustments>Desaturate and then use the Brightness/Contrast command to boost the tones. Go to Filter>Blur>Surface Blur and, using the preview as a guide, select a setting that blurs the fine details but retains the lines. We used a Radius of 4 and a Threshold amount of 12.

03 The sketch edges Duplicate the blurred layer and go to Filter>Stylize>Glowing Edges. You'll want settings that strike an even balance between smooth lines and fine details. You don't want the edges to appear too strong or busy, as a soft sketch effect is the goal. We used an Edge Width of 2, Edge Brightness of 19 and Smoothness of 8.

04 See the effect Now press Cmd/Ctrl+I to invert the colours of the layer. Set the blending mode to Color Burn. Turn off the visibility of the blurred photo layer to fully see the effect. Use some soft brush work on a layer mask attached to the sketch layer to hide any unwanted lines that are left by simply painting them away.

05 Intensify the lines If the sketched lines look too faint, you can intensify the effect by duplicating the sketch layer. If this then makes the effect too strong, pull back on the opacity of the duplicate layer. In our example of the kitten we reduced the Opacity to a mere 37% on the duplicate layer.

06 Shading Turn on the visibility of the blurred photo layer. Change this layer's blending mode to Color Burn and reduce the Opacity to 50%. Hold down Opt/Alt and press the 'Add layer mask' button to hide the entire layer. Use a soft brush with white paint on the mask to reveal areas for the look of shading.

Work smarter

Who needs more history?
Increase your safety net by expanding your history states

Don't you wish life had a Cmd/Ctrl+Z? We all do. Some of you may be saying "I just wish Photoshop let you undo more than one step" (Shhhhh. It does. Hold down Shift with your Cmd/Ctrl+Z and you get 20 steps). If you open up your History palette you can see the last twenty steps you took in Photoshop. You can easily dial back in time clicking on any of those steps to return to that point. But what happens when 20 isn't enough? Those can disappear quickly when you are painting or using any of the other brush-based tools. Fortunately, 20 is just the default setting in Photoshop. It can be easily increased for more peace of mind. Remember, though, that there is a performance trade-off for increased history. Every step of history is another state of the document Photoshop has to keep track of.

01 **Know your history** Go to Edit> Preferences>Performance. Look in the History & Cache section for the History States. The default is 20 but it can go up to 1,000. We don't recommend going that high as it becomes so memory intensive that eventually the program's performance will become painfully slow.

02 **Test it out** Go ahead and press OK to commit to the change and open up a new document. Be sure you have your History palette open as well. Grab the brush (or any other tool for that matter) and begin working. Watch as your History palette fills up to whatever number you set.

03 **Snapshot alternative** In the History palette there's a small camera icon in the footer. Pressing this creates a snapshot of the current state of your document. Clicking on that snapshot will return the document to that state regardless of how many steps have gone by. This serves as an alternative to increasing History states.

Digital art

Delicious HDR toning
Use a single image to get a stunning HDR effect

High Dynamic Range photography is a recent photographic trend that demands notice. Whether you love it or hate it, the effects are impossible to ignore with the ultra vibrant colours and super crisp details. True HDR requires multiple exposures from a camera to capture a higher range of light, hence the term. Exposures are usually bracketed to capture shadow information as well as highlight information, and then all that is compressed down into a single image. Technically, this is impossible to do with a single, limited range photograph. But far be it from us to allow the laws of reality to stand in the way of trying! The effect can be approximated using a single image, in fact Photoshop CS5 has a feature actually named HDR Toning that only allows the use of a single image. The options available in this feature can be overwhelming, so let's break them down.

Use the HDR Toning feature to turn single shots to HDR

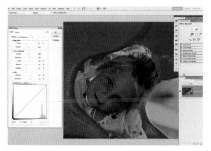

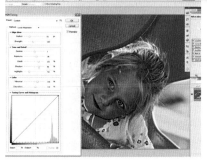

01 **Edge Glow** Open your photo and go to Image>Adjustments>HDR Toning. It's usually best to start with a preset that is close to the effect you have in mind and work from there. We chose the Photorealistic preset to start with for our picture. In the Edge Glow section, the Radius value adjusts the size of the glow and the Strength value adjusts the visibility. We used 51 and 1.82 respectively.

02 **Tone and Detail** In the Tone and Detail area, we suggest starting with the Shadow slider as it will have one of the biggest impacts on the image. We used +44. From there, move to Gamma and Exposure to adjust the brightness, We used 1.00 and .95. We then set the Detail to 122 and Highlight to -51.

03 **Colour adjustment** In the Color section, the Vibrance and Saturation sliders perform similar tasks, but the Vibrance is more concerned with luminous values while the Saturation is more concerned with colour intensity. We used a Vibrance of 6 and a Saturation of 17. If the colours appear off-kilter, a Hue/Saturation adjustment layer can bring them back into line for the perfect HDR effect.

Basic correc

Transform your digital photos with this collection of essential tips and tricks to fix common flaws

Learn to make quick selections

tions

"There's always something new to learn in Photoshop"

60

57

58

Fix any snap with this selection of fail-safe tricks

Sharpen your images using the UnsharpMask tool

Replace colours in your photos quickly and easily

50 PHOTOSHOP TRICKS YOU NEED TO KNOW

We've gathered our favourite image-editing tips that are guaranteed to help you improve your pictures

No matter how long anyone works with Photoshop, there's always something new to learn. Even if you're an image-editing expert, it's impossible to remember every little nook and cranny of Photoshop, and if you're a novice then even some things that may seems basic can be a real revelation and save you hours of head scratching. So, to start this section we've put together ten pages of tips and tricks that will speed up your image editing, give you a whole new bundle of special effects and techniques, and some that might just jog your memory in time for that next deadline-driven graphics project.

So, feast your eyes on this veritable Pandora's Box of Photoshop goodness… it may just save you hours of frustration!

Reflection via layer masks

Tip 1

Create a reflection by adding a simple gradient to a layer mask

Duplicate the image layer containing the object, and flip it via Edit>Transform>Flip vertical. Move the reflection into place using the Move tool ('V'). Add a layer mask, choose the Gradient tool and drag a black-to-white gradient over the bottom half of the layer mask.

Duplicate the object layer to create a copy of it on another layer

Flip the copy, position and add a layer mask. Click on the thumbnail for the Layer Mask

Drag a Black/White gradient vertically over the duplicated object image, via the mask

Tip 2

Terrific Tattoos!

Create stunning realistic digital tattoos with a little help from the Displace filter

Sometimes digital tattoos don't look very convincing, simply because they don't wrap around the body properly. However, by using the Displace filter you can make them really fit the body. First, design your tattoo on a plain white background.

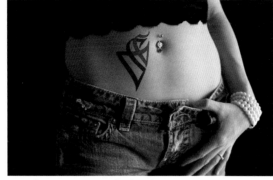

No needles, no regrets – tattoos the Photoshop way

01 Displacement Map
Duplicate your body image. On the duplicate, go to the Channels palette and click the Red channel. Select all and then copy. Return to the Layers palette and paste. Flatten the image and save it as a PSD file, naming it Displace.

02 Paste the tattoo Return to the original body image, open your tattoo image and drag and drop it into the image. Set the blending mode for the tattoo layer to Multiply. Scale and position via Edit>Transform>Scale.

03 Distort Go to Filter> Distort Displace. Enter 15 for both scales and click OK. Locate your Displace file, click on it and click Open. The tattoo will now be wrapped around the body contours. Reduce the layer Opacity a little if needed.

"Increasing Saturation can sometimes blow out colours; try Vibrance instead"

Tip 3

Stay safe with Vibrance

Increasing Saturation can sometimes blow out colours; try Vibrance instead

If you've got an image that lacks saturation in some areas, rather than use the Hue/Saturation command, try using Image>Adjustments> Vibrance. The Vibrance command will increase the saturation of only the colours in your image that need it, rather than increasing saturation globally as the Saturation command does.

Tip 4

Easier Eyedropper

Be sure you pick the colour you really want

In CS5, the Eyedropper tool has a pop-up sampling ring, making choosing colours easier. Activate it via the checkbox in the Options bar.

Tip 5

Easy hair selections

Finally, an easy way to select fly-away hair strands, thanks to the Refine Edge command in CS5

Make a rough selection using the Quick Selection tool. Click on Refine Edge in the Options bar. Add a small amount via the Radius slider and choose the Refine Radius tool. Now brush around the hair outline using this tool at a suitable size. Check Decontaminate Colours and use the slider to remove any vestiges of remaining colour. From Output To: choose New Layer With Layer Mask for perfect results.

Make a rough selection around your subject and let Refine Edge do all of the work

Just brush over the stray hairs using the Refine Radius tool and watch as a perfect hair mask is created for you

Tip 6

Quick Colour info

You don't have to reach for the Eyedropper get a colour reading

Once you have the Info palette on screen (Window>Info), any Photoshop tool will give you a colour reading within the palette.

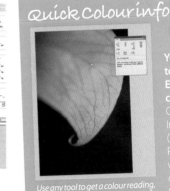

Use any tool to get a colour reading, using Caps Lock to get precise info

Tip 7

Levels without Clipping

Don't risk clipped black and white points when you're busy adjusting Levels. Use the Opt/Alt key as a handy safeguard

Next time you're adjusting the black and white points in your image via the Levels command, hold down the Opt/Alt key as you drag each pointer beneath the Histogram. Stop dragging when you see any clipped areas appearing.

Tip 9

Crop overlays

In CS5, the Crop tool comes complete with a choice of helpful guides

Once you've dragged a crop, go to the Options bar for the Crop tool and choose from Grid or Rule Of Thirds crop guide overlays. The grid can be useful for lining up crops with image elements and Rule Of Thirds is a great compositional aid.

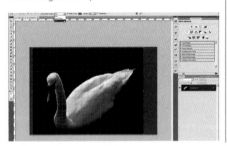

Consistent colour across two images

Tip 8

A simple, overlooked command for harmonising the colours in separate images

Image>Adjustments>Match Color will take the overall colours from one image and apply them to another. Open both the images (the target and source images). Make the target image the active one and go to Image>Adjustments>Match Color. From the Source: option in the Image Statistics section, choose the image you want to take the colours from. If you need to adjust the colour change in the target image, carefully adjust the sliders.

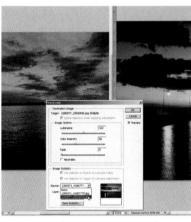

There's no panic if the colours in two images don't match, just use the Match Color command

Apply the colours from your source image to the target image for a quick edit

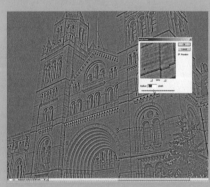

Sharpen up with High Pass

Tip 10

Flexible, non-destructive sharpening via a layer and the High Pass filter

Open your image and duplicate the Background Layer (Cmd/Ctrl+J). On the duplicate layer, go to Filter>Other>High Pass. Set the Radius to around 10 pixels and click OK. Change the blending mode for this layer to Hard Light. Now reduce the Opacity of this layer until you're happy with the result. It's best to zoom into 100% to visually gauge the sharpening effect as you reduce the layer opacity.

Adjust the layer Opacity to control the amount of sharpening that's applied to your image

Clever Curves adjustments

Tip 11

Use the on-screen adjustment tool within the Curves dialog for faster image adjustments

In Photoshop CS4 upwards, you don't have to adjust a curve directly. Choose the on-screen adjustment tool at the bottom right of the Curves dialog and simply click and drag on an area in your image. Drag up to lighten and down to darken!

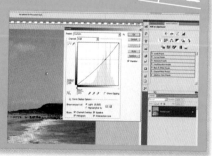

Tip 12

Scrub that!

Don't dial in values within Photoshop, try scrubbing for more speed

Wherever you see a value box, such as the Opacity value in the Layers palette, next to it you'll see a text label. Click and hold on that label and you can 'scrub' rather than fiddling with minute slider pointers.

Just click and drag on that text label to easily scrub through values

Tip 13

Texture overlays

Subtle textures can transform your images in just a few clicks

Copy and paste your texture shot into the image. Go to Edit>Transform>Scale, and use the corner handles to scale the texture to cover the image. Now experiment with blending modes on the texture layer. Overlay, Soft Light and Hard Light work well.

Paste your texture and choose a blending mode. Finish by experimenting with adjusting layer opacity

Tip 15

Correct colour casts

You can easily correct colour casts within the Curves dialog

From the Curves dialog, choose the Grey Eyedropper. Now carefully look for an area in your image which should be neutral in colour. Click on this area with the eyedropper to correct the colour cast in a single click.

Choose the grey eyedropper and click in a part of your image which should be neutral

Tip 14

HDR Toning

You don't need to shoot multiple exposures to create stunning HDR effects in CS5

The great thing about HDR Toning is that you only need a single image, not multiple exposures to create a faux HDR image. Open your image and go to Image>Adjustments>HDR Toning. Creating your effect can be as simple as choosing one of the supplied HDR effects from the Preset: option. Even once you've chosen a preset you can adjust every aspect of the Edge Glow, Tone and Detail or Colour via the sliders within the dialog. It's worth spending a little time adjusting the Detail slider as this will really amplify that classic HDR appearance, and increase the Saturation via the sliders in the Color section. The Toning Curve gives you the opportunity to carefully lighten or darken every tone within the image, just like a normal Curves adjustment.

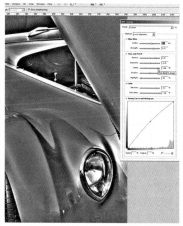

Within HDR Toning, you'll find all the usual HDR adjustments are at your fingertips

> *"The great thing about HDR Toning is that you only need a single image, not multiple exposures, to create an HDR effect"*

Snappy snapshots

Create a quick snapshot effect using layers

Tip 16

 01 Scale the image Double-click the Background layer and go to Edit>Transform>Scale. Hold down the Shift key and resize via one of the corner handles. Hit enter and duplicate this layer (Cmd/Ctrl+J).

02 Fill and scale the border layer Cmd/Ctrl-click the lower layer and go to Edit>Fill, choosing White. Return to Edit>Transform>Scale and Shift-drag a corner handle to size the border. Position the border by dragging within the Bounding Box. Hit Enter to commit the transformation.

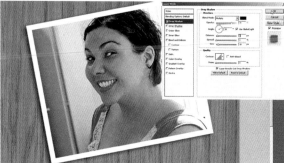

03 Add a shadow and a base Go to Layer>Layer Style, choosing Drop Shadow. Adjust the Distance and Size of the shadow and hit OK. Pasting a wooden texture shot on a layer below these two can really finish the effect off convincingly.

Tip 17
Fast, reusable photo edges

Create and reuse your own photo edges, and drop them over any image
You can create and save black-and-white border files to use again and again. Start with a white document and paint the window for your image with black, carefully creating good-looking edges. Now you can drop this image on to a layer over a photo and set the blending mode to Screen. Resize the layer to fit the image via Edit>Transform>Scale.

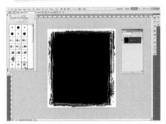

Create a simple black and white image. Try using some Photoshop filters on them

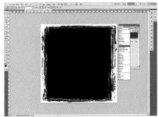

Copy and paste the edge file on a layer over your photo and set the blend mode to Screen

Only the white areas remain, leaving just the edges showing around the image

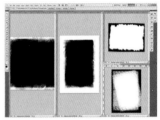

The possibilities are endless, so get creative with edge files and build up a collection!

Tip 18
Tinting black and whites

The Black and White command also has a tinting function
Go to Image>Adjustments> Black and White. Choose one of the Black and White presets, or adjust the sliders to your liking. Now check the Tint check box. Choose the colour of your tint via the Hue slider and adjust its intensity by dragging on the Saturation slider.

Black and white with just a hint of colour, thanks to the Black and White command

Tip 19
Correct perspective

The Lens Correction filter makes correcting perspective wonderfully simple
Go to Filter>Distort>Lens Correction. In the bottom left of the panel, correct vertical perspective by dragging on the slider. You can also correct horizontal perspective with the other slider. Turning the Grid on can help with judging the corrected perspective. Hit OK when you're done to exit the dialog.

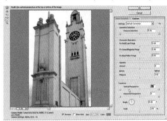

Tip 20
Magical Mini-Bridge!

The Bridge's timesaving little CS5 brother
In Photoshop CS5, you don't have to go use the full-blown version of the Bridge. Simply go to File>Browse in Mini-Bridge and then browse within the workspace.

Tip 21
Mess with Masks

Control layer masks via their own dedicated panel to speed up your masking workflow
When you've created a layer mask, you can Feather it, alter Density or Invert it via the Masks panel. Go to Window>Masks and use the sliders.

Tip 22
The magic of Smart Filters

Smart Filters allow you to change the filter settings again and again
Right-click the layer to filter and choose Convert To Smart Object. Apply your filter in the usual way. Re-edit by double-clicking its smart filter entry attached to the layer.

Tip 23
Super-quick vignettes

Take the super-fast route to effective vignettes
Use the Vignette slider within the Lens Correction filter. Drag it to the left to darken, and to the right to lighten. Control the vignette width with the Midpoint slider.

The Bridge in it's own self-contained Photoshop panel. At last!

Take control of your Layer Masks via Window> Masks and feel the power of the panel

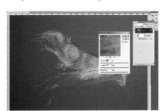

Editable Photoshop filters, all thanks to the versatility of Smart Objects

For classic vignettes, just rely on the sliders within the Lens Correction filter

Tip 24
Add a spotlight for drama

A simple spotlight can add a touch of drama and focus to still life compositions

Duplicate the Background Layer (Cmd/Ctrl+J). Go to Filter>Render>Lighting Effects. Use the default spotlight, sizing and positioning it appropriately. Adjust the darkness around the light by adjusting the Ambience slider.

Use the default spotlight to throw some light on your still life images

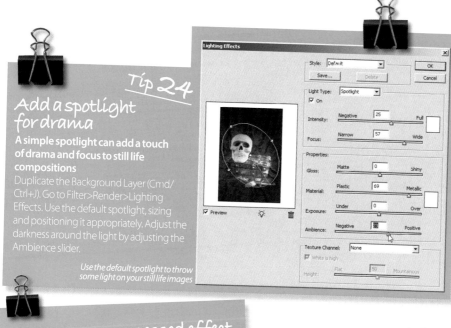

Tip 25
Straighten with the Crop tool

The Crop tool is more versatile than you might think

Choose the Crop tool and choose Grid from the Crop Guide Overlay option in the Options bar. Drag a crop over the image. Now place your cursor outside one of the corners on the Crop Box and drag to rotate the crop, matching the grid up to a horizontal or vertical within the image. Adjust the side handles to your desired crop and hit the Enter key to commit the crop.

Drag a crop, rotate it, adjust and commit. Job done!

Curves cross-processed effect
Tip 26

Make adjustments to each of the colour curves to re-create this classic effect

To create this effect, you need to make specific changes to each of the four curves in the RGB image. Go to Layer>New Adjustment Layer>Curves. Choose the individual curve from the Channels box and place points on each curve and position them by dragging. Refer to the image below to see each curve shape.

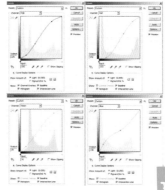
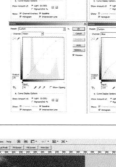

"You can make adjustments to each colour curve to re-create classic photographic effects"

Tip 27
Get creative with Film Grain

Make film grain more adaptable via a filled layer

Use the Grain filter (Filter>Texture>Grain) to add various film grain effects to your images, but use it on a separate layer filled with 50% Gray (via Edit>Fill). Desaturate this layer once you added the grain, and set the blending mode to Soft Light or Overlay. You can adjust the grain intensity simply by modifying the Opacity of this layer.

If you have fond memories of good old-fashioned snapshots, create them yourself in Photoshop

Black and white points in the Curves dialog
Tip 28

You don't have to use Levels to set black and white points... you can also do it in Curves

Drag the lower corner point on the curve to line up with the left-hand end of the histogram. Do the same with the upper-right corner point to correct the white point.

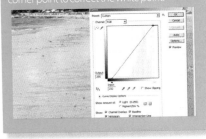

Big Data  Tip 29

Big Data refers to areas of a layer which lie outside the canvas area

Sometimes, you'll have parts of a layer that extend beyond the edges of the canvas. To see these areas, go to Image>Reveal All.

Reveal any 'Big Data' in your image via Image>Reveal All. Now you'll see any previous hidden layer contents

Manage Masks

Don't go to the Channels palette to duplicate a layer mask, just drag-and-drop

To copy a layer mask from one image layer to another, hold down the Opt/Alt key and simply click and drag the mask thumbnail to the other layer.

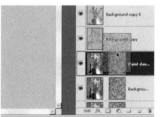

Opt/Alt-click-drag is all that's need to duplicate a mask and add it to another image layer

Paint selections

Don't forget the power of Quick Mask for creating complex selections

Hit 'Q' on the keyboard to enter Quick Mask Mode. Paint the selection with black, erase it with white. Hit 'Q' again to exit.

Quick masks allow you to simply paint complex selections with the humble Brush tool

Precious selections

You'll often use a selection more than once, so make sure to save it

When you created a complex selection, save it via Select>Save Selection. When you want to use it again, go to Select>Load Selection.

Don't risk losing that complex selection, make sure to save it in case you need it in the future

Tip 30

Get creative with Gaussian Blur

Just a simple blur for high-impact fashion shots

Duplicate the Background Layer (Cmd/Ctrl+J). On the duplicate layer set the blending mode to Overlay and go to Filter>Blur>Gaussian Blur choosing a Radius of around 20 pixels. Hit OK to apply the filter. Experiment with other Radius values for a more subtle effect.

For a touch of real pro-studio effects, try a little Gaussian Blur and a simple blending,ode

Type in perspective  Tip 32

Use Vanishing Point to add type in perspective to any plane in your image

Create your type. Go to Select>All, followed by Edit>Copy. Now delete your text layer and add a new layer. Go to Filter>Vanishing Point. Click corner points to create a grid following the plane of the surface. Hit Cmd/Ctrl+V to paste in the text. Now drag the text into the grid and position it wherever you want it along the plane of perspective.

Create your text with the Type tool and then copy it over to the clipboard

Click corner points to create a perspective grid within the Vanishing Point window

Paste the type, drag it into the perspective grid and position it in perspective by dragging

The Vanishing Point filter can work wonders with creating in extreme perspective

Tip 38
Automatic lens correction

Take the guesswork out of correcting lens distortion in CS5

In CS5, you can Auto Correct lens distortion in the Lens Correction filter. Choose the Make and Model of your camera and then choose the appropriate Lens Profiles to correct distortion without any of the guesswork.

Lens Correction now has specific lens profiles built in

Tip 35
Artistic brushed borders

Paint onto a mask to get arty with borders around your images

Duplicate the Background layer (Cmd/Ctrl+J). Fill the original background with a colour of your choice. Via Edit>Transform>Scale, reduce the size of the image on the upper layer a little. Add a mask via Layer>Layer Mask>Reveal All. Now paint around the edges of the image with black at 50% Opacity, making sure to hide any hard edges.

Try different brushes to create an endless variety of artful image borders

Tip 36
Non-destructive Dodging and Burning

Use a simple grey filled layer for damage-free targeted tonal adjustments

Add a new layer, and via Edit>Fill, fill it with 50% Gray. Set the blending mode to Soft Light. Paint with a soft brush at 15% Opacity, using black to gradually darken and white to subtly lighten areas in your image.

You can dodge and burn simply by using the Brush tool with black and white

Tip 37
Neutral Density impact in CS5

You don't need a neutral density filter for your camera… just do it all in Photoshop

Use the new Neutral Density gradient on a layer set to Soft Light to add impact to skies in your landscapes.

The new Neutral Density gradient makes it easy to add impact to skies

> *"Create a simple brush to quickly add copyright tags to your photos"*

Tip 39
Copyright Brush

Create a simple brush to quickly add copyright tags to your photos

Create you text in black, on a white canvas with the Type tool. Crop and Flatten your image. Now go to Edit>Define Brush Preset. Give your new brush a name and hit OK. You'll now find your new brush in the Brush Picker. Use your new brush at any size, with any colour.

Protect your work by creating a quick and simple brush to stamp your copyright information

Content-Aware magic

Use the new Content-Aware features of Photoshop CS5 for seamless clean-ups

CS5 offers users some fantastic new features, top of which are the new Content-Aware options. These allow you to perform nothing short of image-editing alchemy, with Photoshop replacing pixels with other information, meaning you can clone away items in a blink of an eye. Once you get used to how they work, there's no turning back! Here's a look at the two features.

Tip 40

Content-Aware fill

Make a quick selection around the blemish in your image, go to Edit>Fill, choose Content-Aware for Contents and just click OK. Repeat if it doesn't look good the first time.

Content-Aware spot healing

Content-Aware is also available for the Spot Healing Brush in CS5. Just choose it from the Options bar and then brush over objects to remove them. Enjoy the best results ever seen in retouching tools.

Tip 41
Turn down the noise!

Camera RAW is the best choice for Noise Removal, even with JPEG images
In the Bridge, right-click the image and choose Open In Camera Raw. Click the Detail tab. The Luminance slider is use to remove Luminance noise (dark speckles), and the Color slider removes Colour Noise. Detail slider help to keep edges sharp.

Tip 42
Reshape with Puppet Warp

Puppet Warp is a very powerful tool, but knowing how best to use it is the key to success
When you're using Puppet Warp, it's important that you not only place pins to move, but that you first place pins to 'lock down' the parts of the image you want to remain in place and not be affected by the warping. As the walkthrough below shows, using this feature correctly allows you to make very fine, targeted changes, with subtle, undetectable results.

Make your images bend to your whim with the magical Puppet Warp tool

Black, white, and colour
Tip 43

Really mix things up by combining black and white with a splash of colour
The best way to create a selective colour effect is via a layer mask. Go to Layer>New Adjustment Layer>Black And White. Choose one of the Black and White Presets, or adjust the sliders within the black and white panel to create a good, strong black-and-white image. Click on the layer mask attached to the adjustment layer and choose the Brush tool, making sure that Black is your Foreground Color. Now just paint with black wherever you want to restore colour from the background layer beneath. You can hide overpainted areas by painting back into the mask with white.

Use a Black and White adjustment layer to create the overall mono image

Paint on the adjustment layer mask to reveal to colour from the background beneath

01 Lock down Click to place various pins around and within the object to be warped. These 'lock down' pins will prevent other areas of the subject being warped.

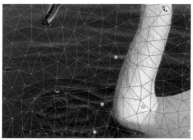

03 Drag to distort Now simply click and drag of the selected pins to distort this particular area of the image. You can select multiple pins by Shift-clicking.

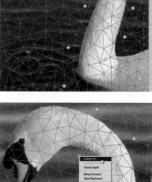

02 Pins for warping Now click to place pins along the feature that you want to bend, warp or adjust. You can activate individual pins simply by clicking on them.

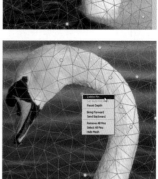

04 Add and subtract layer At any time you can add more pins or delete some. To delete a pin, right-click it and then choose Delete Pin. By carefully controlling where pins are placed you'll be able to producing convincing results.

Tip 44
Adjust multiple layers

Adjust the Opacity and Fill of multiple layers at once
In Photoshop CS5, you can adjust the Opacity of two or more layers at once. Cmd/Ctrl-click multiple layers and adjust the slider

Cmd/Ctrl-click multiple layers before adjusting Opacity or Fill

Classic hand tinting
Create classic hand tinted black-and-white images with the addition of a layer
Add a new layer above your black-and-white image, setting the blending mode to Color. Use a soft brush with your chosen colours to paint over the image, for classic hand tinting.

Tip 45

Add a layer and start painting to add hints of colour to black and whites

Tip 46

Super-fast high key effect

Create a high-key image from the Black channel in CMYK mode
The classic high key effect can work very well for a really modern portrait effect, and by duplicating your image, changing its colour mode and stealing just one channel, you can create this effect quickly and easily.

Duplicate your image (Image>Duplicate). On the duplicate image go to Image>Mode>CMYK. Click on the Channels palette, click on the Black channel, Select All and hit Cmd/Ctrl+C top copy it. Return to your RGB image, and go to Cmd/Ctrl+V to paste. Flatten the image and you're done!

Tip 47

Simple and effective skin smoothing

Use the Median filter to effectively smooth skin
Duplicate the Background layer (Cmd/Ctrl+J). Now go to Filter>Noise>Median. Use a small Radius value, just enough to remove the unwanted skin texture (you'll be able to judge this effect within the preview window). Hit OK to apply the filter. Now, on this smoothed layer, apply a layer mask via Layer>Layer Mask>Hide All. The layer will now be hidden completely. Choose the Brush tool, click directly on the layer mask thumbnail and paint over the skin with white at 75% Opacity, avoiding the eyes, lips and other facial features that don't want the smoothing effect. You can make the final smoothing effect look completely convincing by reducing the opacity of this layer a little.

Don't let exaggerated skin texture spoil your portrait shots

Change specific colours via Hue/Saturation

Tip 48

With Hue/Saturation you can make specific colour changes as well as global ones
In Hue/Saturation, choose any colour from the Colors drop-down. Now choose the eyedropper and click the colour in your image you want to change. Just move the Hue slider to adjust that particular colour.

Quickly alter the colour of an object using the Hue/Saturation command

Choose layers by content

Tip 50

Don't search for a particular layer. Ctrl/Cmd -click to choose it
If you are working on multi-layered documents, finding the one you want can be a nightmare. Choose the Move tool ('V') and Cmd/Ctrl-click on any element in your image to automatically jump to that layer in the Layers palette. Simple!

Cmd/Ctrl-click on any element in your image to select that layer in the Layers palette

Reset, don't cancel

Tip 49

If you make a mistake with an adjustment, don't cancel out of it, just hit Reset
Whenever you're working within a dialog box that has a Cancel button, you can hold down the Opt/Alt key to change this to a Reset button.

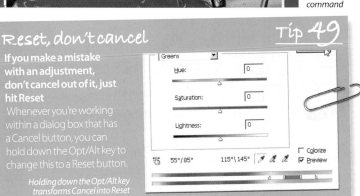

Holding down the Opt/Alt key transforms Cancel into Reset

Correct lens distortion

This frequent photographic snag is solved within just a matter of minutes

Lens distortion is most obvious in architectural photographs, when the top of the building appears to be smaller than the bottom.

You can guarantee this type of distortion when you're not completely square on to your subject. But let's be honest, this is impossible standing at ground level and looking upwards.

You'll also notice lens distortion when using a wide-angle lens to capture something that is supposed to be straight-edged. And that's where Photoshop comes in, with its easy-to-use Lens Correction filter.

If your image appears to be an architectural disaster then you've got a case of lens distortion – this five-minute fix should square-out any problems.

Before

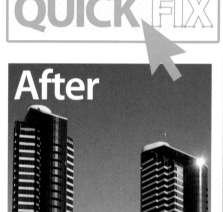
QUICK FIX

After

Top tip: Using grids and guides over the top of your image will show exactly what's straight or wonky.

THE RIGHT PERSPECTIVE
This could well be the fastest photographic solution in history

01 Set up grid Open an image that has plenty of lens distortion and duplicate its layer in the Layers palette. Go to Filter>Distort>Lens Correction in the top menu bar and this will open a new dialog box. Select the Move Grid tool and shift the grid so it sits on an edge of the subject in your image.

02 Straighten up First use the Vertical Perspective slider under Transform to correct the tilt. Try aligning the tilt correction with the grid. Now adjust the Remove Distortion slider at the top right of the box to pinch or expand the pic from its centre. Move between these two sliders for best results, then hit OK.

03 Crop down The edges of the image will now be bowed out of shape. Select the Crop tool and cut these edges out. Spin and resize the cropping area to make the subject as upright as possible. Be prepared to lose areas of the image due to this cropping, but more importantly, your image should now have the right perspective – in under five minutes!

Flip for better composition

Create symmetrical landscapes for striking images

Formal gardens use symmetry to plan planting and make a pleasing composition for the eye, but you can never train nature to conform! And if you have a formal scene, as we have here, any imperfections ruin the dream of a symmetrical composition. But with a spot of selecting, copying, pasting and flipping, you can enjoy the perfect composition you have always dreamt of.

Top tip: Use this technique to expand horizons and make panoramic effects. Simply copy, paste and shift along.

THREE STEPS TO PERFECT SYMMETRY
Be a digital maestro

01 Divide and conquer Open your image and then pick the Rectangular Marquee tool. Zoom into your image so you can see everything and then click and drag to select half of the image. We decided to take the fountain as the centre of the shot and so cut that in half.

02 Copy cat With the selection all selected, go to Edit>Copy and then Edit>Paste. Drag this layer down to the New Layer icon in the Layers palette to duplicate. Click the eye icon next to the Background layer (your original image) to turn it off. That keeps it safe.

03 Flippin' good Ensuring you have the top layer selected, go to Edit>Transform>Flip Horizontal. The selection from Step 1 is now back to front. Go to the Move tool and either hold down Shift and click-drag to the right, or use the arrow keys to nudge it along. Make sure the middle lines up and then bask in the symmetry!

Tips & fixes

Straighten in PS CS5

CS5 users have a dedicated straightening tool. Well, kind of. Open your wonky image and click on the Eyedropper tool in the Toolbar. When the fly-out menu appears, pick the Ruler tool. Click and drag this along an edge that should be straight. Let go, scoot up to the Options bar and click the Straighten button. Your image will be straightened AND cropped. If you want to crop it yourself, simply hold down the Opt/Alt key on your keyboard while you are clicking the Straighten button.

Before

Crop and straighten images

A wonky horizon can easily ruin an image, but it's as easy as pie to sort these out using Photoshop's automated tool

In an ideal world we would always take photos with a tripod carefully set up to ensure that our images were perfectly straight. But, let's face it, when you're out and about and in the middle of a photographic frenzy, worrying about a minor thing like a straight horizon isn't high on the list of priorities. Until you get home, that is, and look through your images and realise every one looks as though its contents are clinging on for dear life to avoid falling out of the frame! It's a particular problem with landscape shots where there is a clear horizon that should be straight and obviously isn't.

Well, worry not, because Photoshop has a tool to sort you out. Actually there are various tools, depending on what version of Photoshop you are using. We are concentrating on the Straighten tool using Photoshop Elements 9, as CS5 now boasts a similar feature. Draw along the area that should be straight and then wait while it is rotated so things are nice and level. Easy peasy.

If you haven't got Elements or CS5, you are not doomed to a lifetime of wonky scenes; there are a couple of options for doing a similar thing, so we'll look at these as well. CS5 is dealt with in the tip box, while earlier versions of Photoshop are examined from Step 4.

STRAIGHTEN HORIZONS WITH PHOTOSHOP ELEMENTS
Make light work of sliding landscapes

01 Set the tool up Open up the image that you need to straighten. The wonky horizon is pretty noticeable – we must have had one leg in a hole! Go to the Toolbar and pick the Straighten tool, then, in the Canvas Options menu, select Crop to Remove Background (earlier versions of Elements will say Trim Background).

02 Drag to straighten The idea is to drag the Straighten tool across an edge that should be straight. Most of the time that will be a horizon line, as is the case here. Zoom in to the image if you need to (Cmd/Ctrl and +) and, starting from the left edge, click and drag the tool across the horizon (keep the mouse button held down)

03 On the straight and narrow As soon as you let go of the mouse button, Elements will present a lovely straightened image for you, all nice and trim. If you'd rather crop away excess yourself, simply select Crop to Original Size (this appears as simply Original Size in earlier versions of Elements) from the Canvas Options area.

04 In CS or above As mentioned, it is possible to straighten images in full versions of Photoshop. One way to do this is with the Measure tool. This is hiding behind the Eyedropper, so click on that in the Toolbar to get the fly-out menu. Select the Measure tool and then click and drag across and edge that should be straight.

05 Rotate the canvas Go to Image>Rotate Canvas>Arbitrary to call up a window. An angle will be automatically entered – this comes from the line you drew with the Measure tool. Photoshop will also have worked out which way your image needs to rotate. Click OK and then use the Crop tool to trim the edges.

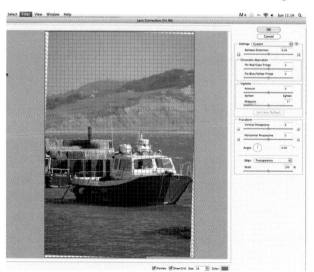

06 Straighten with Lens Correction Another way of straightening images in pre-CS5 versions of Photoshop lies within the Filters menu. Go to Filter>Distort>Lens Correction. This will call up a new window. Go over to the left-hand side and pick the Straighten icon (second one down).

07 Draw across the horizon With the tool selected, click and drag across an edge that should be straight (is this starting to sound familiar?). As soon as you let go of the mouse, Photoshop will whip your image around so the horizon is straight.

Content-Aware Scaling

An intelligent method of selectively resizing images

Content-Aware Scaling came into Photoshop in version CS4. It's grouped with the Transform tools and acts in the same way, but with a bonus.

Found in the Edit menu, Content-Aware Scaling not only resizes your image but also keeps the main subject at its original size. It resizes all the other areas that have no distinct subject. When you use the Free Transform tool in Photoshop to adjust an image's size, the entire contents are affected. Content-Aware Scaling recognises areas of similarity such as sky or grass, and only resizes these.

If an image has more than one main subject, for example a portrait of a group of people, the areas lying between each person are resized. However, this isn't always perfect every time, as Content-Aware Scaling can produce rough patches. This is where some pixels haven't been blended smoothly, so there are limits to the extent of rescaling. It all changes depending on the subject you're dealing with.

Using this technique to resize an image saves possible hours of painstaking cropping, copying and cloning. Combine Content-Aware Scaling with selections saved as alpha channels, and you can protect areas against any distortion.

Read through this guide to discover a solution to distortion caused by Content-Aware Scaling and how best to use this essential feature in Photoshop.

Where is it? Content-Aware Scaling can be found in the Edit menu just above the other Transform tools such as Free Transform. Its job is the same, but it keeps the dimensions of the main subjects in your image.

After

Content-Aware Scaling
A fast way to resize

Content-Aware Scaling is only available in CS4 onwards, and is an alternative to the Free Transform tool. If you're looking to reshape an image to fit a certain frame without distorting the main subjects, Content-Aware Scaling is made to do just that. It's located under Edit>Content-Aware Scale. Your image is given markers on all four of its corners and sides to show the boundary. By tweaking the settings in the Options bar it can be set to specific dimensions, to protect skin tones and to adjust the amount of distortion. By making selections around subjects you can prevent them being distorted. Practise the three steps on the next page to learn how to use Content-Aware Scaling with a new alpha channel.

Quick Mask mode
Multiple methods of selection

Select the Magic Wand tool and make a selection around your subject. Enter Quick Mask mode by clicking on the thumbnail at the bottom of the toolbar, then using the Brush and Eraser tools you can make your selection more accurate. Experiment with other selection methods – for example try using the Magnetic Lasso tool, which sticks to the edges of your subject as you run it around the edges. Try the Pen tool to create a smoother selection by joining points along an edge. You can then resize these parts or save the selection (Select>Save Selection).

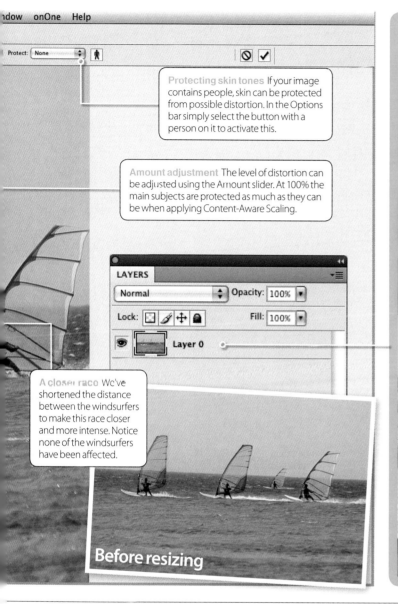

Protecting skin tones If your image contains people, skin can be protected from possible distortion. In the Options bar simply select the button with a person on it to activate this.

Amount adjustment The level of distortion can be adjusted using the Amount slider. At 100% the main subjects are protected as much as they can be when applying Content-Aware Scaling.

A closer race We've shortened the distance between the windsurfers to make this race closer and more intense. Notice none of the windsurfers have been affected.

Before resizing

Making Alpha channels

Content Aware Scaling can work with alpha channels to protect an area from distortion. They save a selection for repeated use, great for protecting many subjects at once.

01 Make a selection Use the Quick Selection tool to select the main subject. Use a small brush for trickier areas, and use the Magic Wand tool to select multiple subjects in your image.

02 Save your selection When the selection is complete, head to Select>Save Selection. In the dialog box name your selection and hit OK. Open the Channels palette and you'll see it saved there. Hit Cmd/Ctrl+D.

03 Locate the selection Go to Edit>Content-Aware Scale, and in the Options bar, under Protect, select the name of the channel just made. Now when you resize your image the channel won't become distorted.

Protect skin tones
Designed for portraits

Content-Aware Scaling has an option to retain quality and shape in skin tones In portrait images. This is ideal if you want to retain the background in a portrait that has a landscape orientation and you need to change it to portrait. Select the option from Edit>Content-Aware Scale, and in the Options bar click on the button shaped as a person.

This protects a person's face from distortion and looking blocky from overlapping pixels. It also saves you making a selection around a person each time you want to resize with Content-Aware Scaling.

Minimise distortion
Improving the look of resizing

To minimioc any distortion when you use Content-Aware Scaling, simply adjust the Amount slider in the Options bar at the top of the Photoshop interface. With a value of 100% the adjustment is more considerate towards

the main subject in your image. However, if you set this to a lower value such as 10%, the main subject and background will both be squashed and moved out of shape. Try to experiment with different values to achieve the correct level of distortion for your particular image.

Control Hue, Saturation and Lightness

This clever command can be used to powerful effect for enhancing colours in your artwork

Tips & fixes

Helping hand

In Photoshop CS4 and CS5 the Hue/Saturation menu contains a helpful tool for changing the saturation of a chosen colour. All that's required is to click on a colour in your image and to drag left or right to remove or add saturation.

One of the many colour adjustment tools featured in Photoshop, the Hue, Saturation and Lightness sliders are accurate ways for boosting or removing colours. Found under Image>Adjustments, the controls in this command can be used for creating different effects, from sepia toning to boosting the red subjects in your image.

We take a look at a couple of these effects using the Hue and Saturation adjustments. The Hue slider, for example, can be used to adjust the entire colour range of an image, or just a small area of selected colour in your image. That's exactly what we've done in the step-by-step over the page, also employing layer masks for tweaking multiple subjects.

The Saturation control changes the intensity of colours, or can be used for removing colour altogether. This is an effective method of converting an image to black and white, without losing tonal detail. It is popular with photographers looking to quickly remove colour, or for creating a selective black and white effect.

Mastering all three adjustments can bring dramatic changes to your artwork. They can help bring more focus to a subject's colour to make it stand out from the rest.

Selective black and whites
Reduce or intensify saturation

Inside the Hue/Saturation menu is a list of colour channels in your image. These can be individually selected for editing, whether it's increasing saturation or turning black and white. It's a fast method of experimenting with different looks.

01 Select tool Open the Hue/Saturation menu by going to Image>Adjustments. Click on the drop-down menu of colour channels. Change the channel to a specific colour, such as Yellow.

02 Remove colour Reduce the Saturation slider to -100 to remove all signs of colour. The range of colours affected, as well as yellow, is shown at the bottom of the menu between the two coloured bars.

03 Adding other colours To intensify or desaturate other colours in your image, choose a different colour in the drop-down list, and manipulate the Saturation. Master will affect all colours in your image.

Hue, Saturation or Lightness?
Three sliders to adjust light and colour

When you open the command, you're presented with three sliders: Hue, Saturation and Lightness. Knowing how each one affects your image will save a lot of potential undoing. The Hue adjustment shifts the entire colour range, which can create peculiar results; the Saturation adjustment reduces the strength of colour in your image, and can result in completely black-and-white images. The last adjustment, Lightness, adds either black or white to colours for a lighter colour range. All three adjustments, however, can be applied to a specific colour instead of the entire image, making these adjustments even more versatile.

Selective colour adjustment
Picking out a colour to enhance

The Hue/Saturation command contains a list of colour channels, as well as an option adjust all colour channels (Master). If your image is of a sunset, for example, you may want to boost the red/orange colour on the horizon, or change the colour of the sunset altogether. By selecting Red from the list of channels in the menu, you can shift the Hue slider to change only the red subjects. The changes may be subtle, but when viewed as a whole, the difference is very noticeable. Selecting colour individually creates more contrast between subjects and makes your image look more dramatic.

TOOL
TRICKS

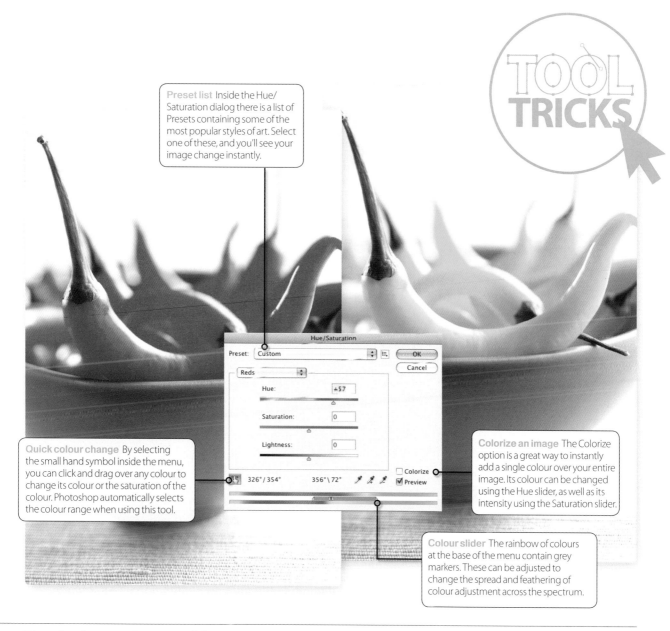

Preset list Inside the Hue/Saturation dialog there is a list of Presets containing some of the most popular styles of art. Select one of these, and you'll see your image change instantly.

Quick colour change By selecting the small hand symbol inside the menu, you can click and drag over any colour to change its colour or the saturation of the colour. Photoshop automatically selects the colour range when using this tool.

Colorize an image The Colorize option is a great way to instantly add a single colour over your entire image. Its colour can be changed using the Hue slider, as well as its intensity using the Saturation slider.

Colour slider The rainbow of colours at the base of the menu contain grey markers. These can be adjusted to change the spread and feathering of colour adjustment across the spectrum.

Replacing colours with one tone
Colorize artwork

The Hue/Saturation menu has the option Colorize. By ticking its box, your image loses all colours present with a single tone. Sliding the Hue adjustment changes this tone to create an abstract look to your artwork. The Saturation slider can also be put to good use in this effect, altering the intensity of the Colorize tone. Colorize is useful for creating a traditional cyanotype image, using a blue from the Hue adjustment slider. Highlights are tinted blue, as well as shadows shifting in colour. It's also great for creating sepia-toned images.

Colour pickers
Adjust a colour with the eyedropper

The menu is supplied with three colour pickers, or more commonly known as 'eyedroppers'. These eyedroppers become active when a colour channel is selected other than Master. The main Eyedropper tool will pick out any colour clicked on, so it can be adjusted. The two other eyedroppers are Add to Sample and Subtract from Sample, indicated with plus and minus symbols. These are useful for adding or removing a colour into the mix after making an adjustment. The colour range affected by adjustments is shown within the dark grey bar next to the two coloured bars.

FROM ONE COLOUR TO THE NEXT
How to alter colour separately across your image

01 **Make selection** Duplicate the background layer to work non-destructively. Choose the Quick Selection tool, or the selection method of your choice, and set its Diameter to 50px. Make sure Auto-Enhance is ticked in the Options bar.

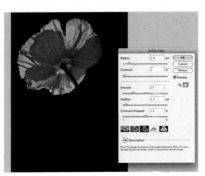

02 **Select first object** With the Quick Selection tool, click and drag a selection over your subject. Click on the Refine Edge menu in the Options bar, and set Feather to 1.5px, Expand to +3 and Radius to 2.9px. This will change depending on the image you are using.

03 **Add layer mask** With the selection active and the duplicated background layer highlighted, click on the Add Layer Mask button in the Layers palette. This separates the particular subject from the rest of the image. Now hit Cmd/Ctrl+D to remove the selection.

04 **Manipulate Hue** On the duplicated background layer, click on the image's thumbnail instead of the layer mask's. Go to Image>Adjustments>Hue/Saturation, and slide to the Hue slider to your desired new colour.

05 **Adjust another** Duplicate the background once more and place below the previous duplicate layer. Using the Quick Selection tool, select another subject to alter. Apply the same Refine Edge command and hit Add Layer Mask button. Hit Cmd/Ctrl+D.

06 **Multi-coloured** Go into the Hue/Saturation adjustment again and adjust the Hue slider to give this subject a change of colour. The layer above this won't be affected, and both subjects can now be adapted separately.

Useful presets
Already prepared effects to use

Photoshop has a number of preset effects inside the Hue/Saturation adjustment menu. These allow you to apply effects quickly, and you can even adjust them further to suit your own image. The list of presets includes Cyanotype, Increase Saturation, Yellow Boost and Old Style. Presets help you achieve popular effects, but you can even save your own from

inside the menu to reuse on future artwork. Next to the OK button, another set of options exists: Save, Load and Delete Current Preset. This gives you control over what you want to do with your favourite effects; you just have to remember to hit Save before clicking on OK!

Quick before/after
Using Preview to your advantage

The Preview option in the dialog window can stay on all the time, so you can see any changes applied in real-time. However, when you think you've tweaked the Hue, Saturation and Lightness sliders for the perfect effect, flick the Preview option on and off and you can see

the before and after versions of your image. This way there's no need to hit OK and then 'undo' if you change your mind. It's also good practice to duplicate the image's layer before applying these effects. Alternatively, apply Hue/Saturation as a new adjustment layer inside the Layers palette. That way you can make a quick retreat if anything goes wrong.

Rescue dull shots with Brightness/Contrast

Get to grips with this useful command and pump some life back into bleak photos

I t doesn't matter if you haven't got elaborate light setups, reflectors and all sorts – you can still take good photos at home. Even if, at first glance, the results are decidedly dodgy. Take our example shot here. This was taken by a window (it was a cloudy day), with no other light source and no tripod. It looks too dark to be of any use, but if we bring the Brightness/Contrast command into play we can tease out the colours and tones to end up with a vibrant shot that could have been taken in a professional studio.

Top tip: Use this technique on any of your indoor shots. If you find yourself sticking to the same settings, record it as an action or turn into a droplet to run on batches of images.

Before

After

QUICK FIX

FROM SHADOWY TO SPRIGHTLY
Coax the colour and contrast out from the shadows

01 **More brightness** Open up your image and then head up to Image>Adjustments>Brightness/Contrast. Move the Brightness slider to +28. Things look better already – tonally flat, but better.

02 **Contrast time** Brightness is for livening up the image and needs to be teamed with contrast to add depth and interest. Move the Contrast slider to +15 to do exactly this. Don't go too far, though, otherwise the highlights will blow. Click OK when done.

03 **Add some zing** The darkness has been wafted away but we can still introduce more colour to the image. Go to Image>Adjustments once more and pick Hue/Saturation. Select Reds from the Channel drop-down menu and move the Saturation slider to the right then choose Yellows and do the same. Much better!

Quick Mask

Discover this versatile tool, which is great for making selections

The Quick Mask mode is one of the most versatile tools you are likely to find within Photoshop's expansive toolbox. Its primary use is for isolating areas that you want left untouched by any adjustments or tweaks.

Quick Mask mode has been around since Photoshop 6.0 and offers a fantastic alternative to the traditional Selection tools. If you find yourself more partial to using the Paintbrush rather than the fiddly Pen tool, then this could well become your ideal selection method.

The Quick Mask mode is activated by clicking on the square icon that contains a white circle. This is situated at the bottom of the toolbar alongside the Standard mode (a white box with a white circle). For instant access, you can simply hit the letter 'Q' on your keyboard and Quick Mask mode activates.

This is a fantastic feature to help in the creation of a whole host of effects. Use it to create quick and easy vignettes for your portraits, paint a Quick Mask on specific colours to achieve amazing selective colouring results, or simply use it to protect an area from an image adjustment you're about to perform.

If you've never used this feature before, we're certain it will be in constant use from this day forward!

Isolating objects

The Quick Mask mode is a fantastic way to select objects or people within a scene. It's not as fiddly as the Pen tool and is easily erased if you make a mistake...

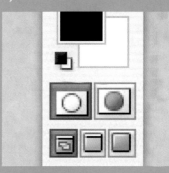

01 **Activate** Open up an image in Photoshop and hit 'Q' to select the Quick Mask mode. You can also activate it by choosing the grey box with a white circle at the bottom of the toolbar.

02 **Brush it on** Select the Brush tool from the toolbar ('B') and choose a suitable size using the square bracket keys. Paint over everything you don't need, using the Eraser if you make any mistakes.

03 **Enjoy** Now deactivate the Quick Mask by hitting 'Q'. You'll have an isolated selection highlighted by marching ants. You are now free to move this selection, cut it, copy it and generally do as you wish!

Change the options
Alter the workings of the mask

The colour of the mask can often be hard to see against the other colours in your image. If this is the case, simply double-click on the Quick Mask icon and a dialog box will appear. Choose a mask colour and mask opacity here. You will also be presented with two display options: Masked Areas and Selected Areas. The Masked Areas option sets your masked areas to black (opaque).

Simply paint with more black to add to the mask. Paint with white to add to your selected area instead. The Selected Areas option is the opposite – masked areas are white (transparent) and selected areas are black.

Control the mask
Use brushes for a feathered effect

For extra control when applying a Quick Mask, you can mix and match the hardness of your brushes. This is ideal for when you want to cut out a picture of an animal, for example. Opt for a soft brush to trace the fur, and choose a harder brush to mask out the more defined features. The soft brush

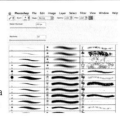

acts as a feather effect and means your final cutout will be less harsh along the edges. These brush-swapping antics can all be performed within one Quick Mask session, giving you ultimate control at speed. This is a far more accurate way of cutting out, compared to using the Lasso for selections.

Get control with brushes You can use any brush to apply a Quick Mask. We recommend you use a soft brush for details such as hair and fur – this will give you a softer, more subtle selection.

Colour your mask If the colour of your mask is too similar to the colours within your image, double-click on the Quick Mask icon. Now click on the Color swatch and select a colour. You can adjust the opacity here as well.

Quick Mask settings To reverse the way the mask operates, just double-click on the Quick Mask icon and select Masked Areas (masked areas are black) or Selected Areas (masked areas are white).

Match Color The Match Color tool is found in Image>Adjustments>Match Color. Ensure that both your images are open in Photoshop first, before selecting this tool. Once selected, use the dialog box to create your settings.

Dialog Hit Match Color and this box appears. Use the drop-down Source menu to select your source image. Ensure Preview is checked to see the change, and use the Luminance, Color Intensity and Fade sliders to adjust.

Selective colouring
Use Quick Mask to pop colours

Selective colouring is a fantastic way to make a dramatic statement in your images especially in portraits. By applying a Quick Mask to an area of colour you wish to preserve, you can then desaturate the remaining portion (Image>Adjustments>Desaturate). Your masked area will retain the original colour and will look striking against the black and white background. Alternatively, you can desaturate your image first and then isolate specific parts of it, which you can colourise. This is ideal for old and new photos alike, and is a super-fast effect that you can play with to perfection.

Quick Mask tips
The little things you should know

A handy tip to know is that you can make a selection with any of your favourite Selection tools and then hit 'Q' to change the selection into a mask. Another top hint – once you have applied a mask, hit 'Q' to leave the Quick Mask mode,

and your selection will appear in the form of marching ants. Move this to a new layer by pressing Cmd/Ctrl+J. For a quick way to invert your mask, simply press Cmd/Ctrl+I. Another gem, when trying to mask fiddly areas, is to switch to the Pencil tool for extra precision. In fact, any of the painting tools can be used when creating a Quick Mask.

Magic Wand tool

Discover this versatile tool, which is great for making selections

Most people associate magic wands with magicians and their showmanship, but Photoshop has its own Magic Wand tool, and it's not used for pulling rabbits out of hats.

The Magic Wand tool is one of Photoshop's main Selection tools, and it's a handy way to customise your selections. It works by sectioning off particular colours inside your image. The selection process is affected by a collection of adjustment options. In this detailed tool guide we give you a rundown of the most important adjustments to remember.

The most effective way to use the Magic Wand tool is to zoom in to your image close enough to see each pixel. Then the four Selection adjustments – New, Add, Subtract and Intersect – can be used with more precision.

The Select menu at the top of Photoshop contains all its hidden adjustments, which affect the way the tool behaves. These options range from a collection of Modify adjustments, a Transform Selection option, and among many others, both Grow and Similar adjustments are found under the Select menu.

This comprehensive selection tool can be used for separating two or more subjects, or singling out specific colours. With all these adjustments and modifications, you can't put a foot wrong making selections with Photoshop's Magic Wand tool. Let's have a look at how to use it!

Making a selection
The Magic Wand is highly versatile and is used to separate areas of colour. In this three-stepper we make sure you tick every box when selecting with this tool.

01 **Set Tolerance** Select the Magic Wand in the toolbar. In the Options bar, set Tolerance to 32 to select a small area of colour. Tick Anti-Alias and Contiguous, but leave Sample All Layers unchecked.

02 **Select the area** Click in the area of colour you want to mark off using the Magic Wand. In the Options bar are four square thumbnails: New, Add, Subtract and Intersect. Use these to make your selection.

03 **New channel** Ctrl/right-click in your selection with the Magic Wand, and pick Save Selection in the list. Give it a name, hit OK and open the Channels palette to find your saved selection.

Quick Mask mode
An accurate way to select

A selection is represented by a black and white dotted line, also known as 'marching ants'. Another way to view the marching ants is in Quick Mask mode. Select the Edit In Quick Mask Mode button at the bottom of the toolbar, and watch the selection change into a light-red colour cast. This colour cast allows you to see the selection in more detail, and you can add or subtract pixels easily in this

mode. With the Brush and Eraser tools, you can paint or erase the colour cast to alter the selection. Click on the Quick Mask Mode icon inside the toolbar to return to Standard editing mode, and to see the marching ants.

Adjust Tolerance
Increase the spread of a selection

The Magic Wand tool works by selecting pixels of a similar colour, and it comes equipped with a Tolerance adjustment. The Tolerance of the Magic Wand tool decides how much of your image a selection will cover. The Tolerance is preset to

32, but you can easily change this to suit the size of the area you want to pick out. Just enter an amount into the Tolerance adjustment box to change it. The bigger the number, the larger the area it covers. With the Tolerance set to 32, a selection spreads across only a small area of a certain colour.

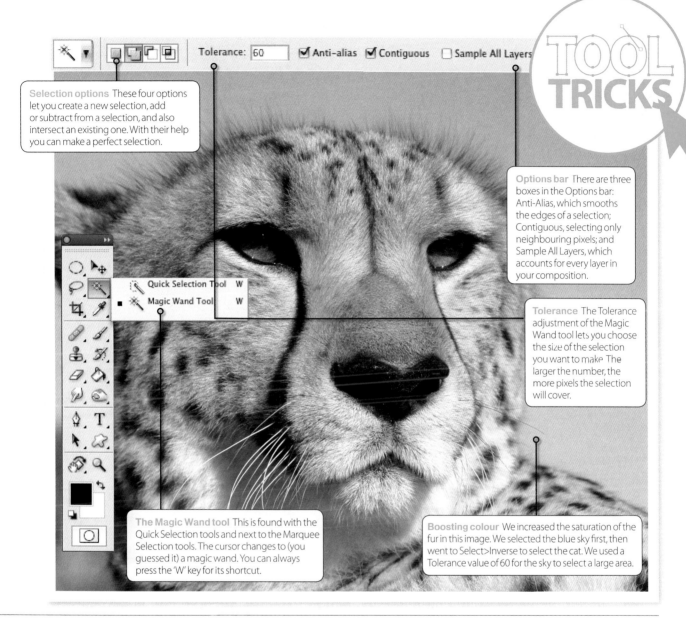

TOOL TRICKS

Selection options These four options let you create a new selection, add or subtract from a selection, and also intersect an existing one. With their help you can make a perfect selection.

Tolerance: 60   ☑ Anti-alias   ☑ Contiguous   ☐ Sample All Layers

Quick Selection Tool   W
Magic Wand Tool   W

Options bar There are three boxes in the Options bar: Anti-Alias, which smooths the edges of a selection; Contiguous, selecting only neighbouring pixels; and Sample All Layers, which accounts for every layer in your composition.

Tolerance The Tolerance adjustment of the Magic Wand tool lets you choose the size of the selection you want to make. The larger the number, the more pixels the selection will cover.

The Magic Wand tool This is found with the Quick Selection tools and next to the Marquee Selection tools. The cursor changes to (you guessed it) a magic wand. You can always press the 'W' key for its shortcut.

Boosting colour We increased the saturation of the fur in this image. We selected the blue sky first, then went to Select>Inverse to select the cat. We used a Tolerance value of 60 for the sky to select a large area.

Magic Wand adjustments
Experiment with Grow and Similar

Once a selection is made you can change it in two ways. Grow and Similar are both found under the Select menu, or you can Ctrl/right-click anywhere inside a selected area to find them in a drop-down menu. Grow makes the selection gradually bigger and will select the same colours. The Similar adjustment picks out all the colours that are similar to the ones already inside your initial selection, but it jumps to any part of your image that is similar. Similar is ideal for selective black and white techniques.

Save a selected area
Create new channels with the Magic Wand

When you save a selection as a new channel, you can adjust it any way you like at any stage. To save a selection, go to Select>Save Selection. In the dialog box, set the Document option to your current image and give the channel a new name. Hit OK, and the new channel will appear in the Channels palette. By selecting its layer, you can then use the Brush or Eraser tools to add or subtract the selection. It works in a similar way to the Quick Mask mode.

Tips & fixes

Stock, textures and inspiration

All the pictures and textures used in this tutorial came from the stock.XCHNG website (**www.sxc. hu**). This is a great resource for free stock images and textures to use in your own projects. We can also use grunge brushes within our projects – these are useful for adding additional texture. You'll find **www. brusheezy.com/ brushes?search= grunge** very helpful here. For help on installing brushes take a look at **www. brusheezy.com/ videos**. For some inspiration for your own projects pop over to **www. designzzz.com/ amazing-grunge- artworks-alex/**.

Make quick selections

Transform photos by selecting parts of photos and then layer them up for a grunge effect

When we talk about grunge in terms of art we refer to dirty textures and faded colours, often with a macabre theme and quality. Using dark tones and white space to emphasise a picture's message, grunge has steadily become a popular form of art.

The artist David Carson, who used non-mainstream photographic techniques and experimental typography to produce his own 'dirty' signature style, is often referred to as 'the father of grunge'. While working as art director on a number of magazines, including *Ray Gun*, Carson developed layouts that often included distorted mixes of typeface and fractured images.

We can use Photoshop to produce dark grunge-inspired photomanipulations using a combination of blending modes, brushes and textures. In this tutorial we won't be using any custom brushes, but will spend our time focusing on manipulating a stock photo of a sunflower with textures and adjustment layers. The tools we'll use are the layer blending modes, Quick Selection tool, Marquee selections, Levels, Selective Color adjustment layer, Hue/Saturation adjustment layers, masks and clipping masks. But it's really not as hard as it sounds!

On the internet there are many free Photoshop grunge brushes available for you to download and install. We will explore some of these as well as alternative textures and inspirational pictures.

GRAB YOUR MOUSE AND IMAGES...

It's time to delve into the world of grunge

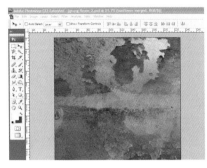

01 Open your files We start our project by finding and opening a nice textured background. This will be the base for our grunge picture that we'll build upon. Next, we find a sunny image of a sunflower and open that up too.

02 Quick Selection tool Locate the Quick Selection tool in the toolbar – it may be hidden behind the Magic Wand tool. You can quickly cycle through the tools by holding Opt/Alt and left-clicking the icons in the toolbox. Now we want to set up the tool in the Options bar, which is found at the top of the screen.

03 It's a setup In the Options bar select the Add To Selection option, which looks like the Quick Selection tool with a plus symbol above it. Also set up Brush Size to around 50 pixels. Make sure that Auto-Enhance is ticked. Now start to paint over the petals of the sunflower to select them; stop frequently to let the selection catch up.

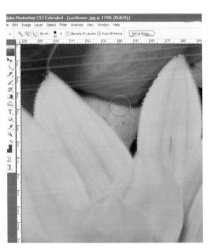

04 Mistakes happen Carry on with the selection, moving inwards so you also choose the stigma (the centre of the flower). If by accident you select something outside the flower, you can easily remove this by using the Subtract From Selection option – it looks the same as Add To Selection but with a minus symbol. Carefully click/paint over the parts you don't want.

05 Copy and paste Copy the flower (Edit>Copy) into your grunge document above the background layer (Edit>Paste), and place it in the centre of the picture. Name this layer 'Sunflower'. Next, add a Levels and Selective Color adjustment layer above the Sunflower layer. The adjustment layers can be found by going to Image>Adjustments in the toolbar.

06 Promotion Select both adjustment layers; promote them to a clipping layer on the Sunflower layer (Layer>Create Clipping Mask). Open Levels and make the Input Levels read 0, 1.54, 255. Open the Selective Color adjustment layer; hit Yellow. Move the Cyan, Magenta, Yellow sliders left so they read -100%.

07 Merge Select the three layers (Levels, Color adjustment, Sunflower) and merge via Cmd/Ctrl+E. Name it 'Sunflower Merged'. As in step 5, add and clip a Levels adjustment layer. Set the Input levels to 0,0,63,255. Use a soft-edged brush with colour set to Black and randomly mask some dark colour.

LET'S FINISH OUR GRUNGE PROJECT
Add some nice textures and more adjustment layers

08 Grunge and masks Open a grungy texture, drag it into the flower picture and name this layer 'Grunge'. Place it over the sunflower so it covers it. Next, select the Rectangle Marquee tool and draw a square-shaped selection over the texture. Finally, add a layer mask to the Grunge layer – Layer>Layer Mask>Reveal Selection.

09 Copycat Change the blending mode of the Grunge layer to Color Burn and reduce the Opacity to 53%. Next, Cmd/Ctrl-click the mask of the Grunge layer, bringing up a selection. Go to the Sunflower Merged layer and add a Reveal Selection mask, as in the previous step.

10 Spiral shell Finally, we open a shell image, and using the Elliptical Selection tool draw around the tip of the shell. Now feather the selection by 50 pixels – Select>Modify>Feather. Copy the selection and paste it back into the flower picture, then place it over the centre of the flower. Name this layer 'Shell'.

11 Cutting corners Copy the Shell layer by pressing Cmd/Ctrl+J together, and place it in the top left-hand corner of the picture. Flip it horizontally by selecting the new layer and going to Edit>Transform> Flip Horizontal. Repeat this for all of the corners.

Layer structure
How we got our grunge look

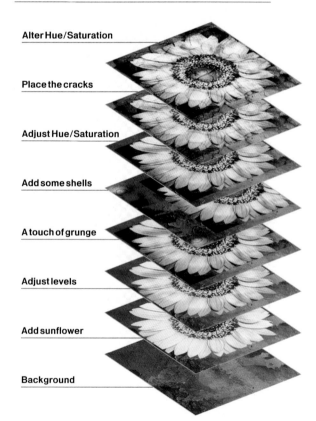

- Alter Hue/Saturation
- Place the cracks
- Adjust Hue/Saturation
- Add some shells
- A touch of grunge
- Adjust levels
- Add sunflower
- Background

12 New hues Merge all the Shell layers together by selecting them in the Layers palette and pressing Cmd/Ctrl+E. Now add a Hue/Saturation adjustment layer and clip it to the Shell layer. Set Saturation to -92 and Lightness to -3.

13 Showing the cracks Finally, open a photo of some good cracks, and place it at the top of your layer stack, then name this layer 'Cracks'. In the Layers palette set the blending mode to Soft Light. At the top of your stack make a new Hue/Saturation adjustment layer, click Colorize and set Hue to 24, Saturation to 93 and Lightness to 2.

Making a magic selection

Discover how to the Magic Wand can make selections in a flash

The Magic Wand is the ideal tool when dealing with objects that have an irregular edge that is hard to manually select, or an image that has a lot of the same colours. It can either select the part of the image you want, or the area outside the part you want and the selection can be inverted. This quick fix tutorial will show you what effect options such as Tolerance, Anti-alias and Contiguous selection have on the process.

Before

QUICK FIX
After

Top tip: If you are cutting out a selection it's worth zooming in to check the edges. If they are too rough it can either need smoothing, modifying or anti-aliasing, which feathers the edges. Click on the Refine Edge button to access the various options.

WAVING THAT MAGIC WAND
Accurate selections in seconds

01 **Set the Tolerance** Load your image and select the Magic Wand tool. It works by selecting areas of similar colour based on the Tolerance setting. Click outside the flower. If not enough of the area has been selected, increase the Tolerance to pick up similar colours. If parts of the image you don't want with the selection are picked up, reduce the Tolerance setting to 20.

02 **Contiguous colours** The Contiguous setting means that it includes similar colours that are next to the ones selected. This is the setting we want for this image because there are similar colours in the middle. If this box is unticked, similar colours are selected wherever they are. Hold down the Shift key and click in areas not selected yet.

03 **Zoom in** Until you zoom in to 100%, you won't see small areas that have been missed. Hold down Shift and click on these. If areas that are not wanted become selected, hold Opt/Alt and click on them to deselect, then reduce the Tolerance. Go to Select>Modify>Smooth and enter a value of 1px to help smooth out any rough edges.

TOOL TRICKS

The Extract filter

Learn how this filter can be used to remove subjects – all it takes is a steady hand

The Extract filter has been around in Photoshop since version 5.5, making it a well-established feature. The filter adds to the existing wide choice of selection methods presented in the toolbar (this is found in the Filters menu). It's yet another option, and like all selection methods, suits only certain types of subjects.

However, it's the Refine Edge command (first appearing in CS3) that has pushed the filter out of sight in CS4 and in the latest version, CS5. If you're using an earlier version than CS3, you won't be able to use the Quick Selection tool or the Refine Edge commands. This is where the Extract filter comes into play. The filter requires you to paint around the edges of a subject with what's called the Edge Highlighter tool, and you then fill an area with paint. The filled area is what you end up with.

Extracting large complex subjects isn't one of the filter's stronger points, and neither is extracting around areas where there's little contrast. For large subjects, it's a timely process painting around every edge at a very close magnification. Where we found the filter most helpful was for picking out small parts of an image quickly – and it does this very effectively.

Read on to find out to access the filter in CS4 and CS5, and how to use it for making quick selections.

Select hair with the Extract filter

Selecting hair in Photoshop has never been an easy task, but the Extract filter does a pretty good job. Here's how to mask hair with the filter and its tool

01 Duplicate and open Duplicate your layer in the Layers palette to work non-destructively. To open the Extract command, go to Filter>Extract, and you should be presented with a large window with your image in it.

02 Create outline In the Extract menu, zoom into your image a couple of times and use the Edge Highlighter tool to paint over the edges. When you reach the strands of hair, make sure your brush covers the frizzy areas.

03 Make the final adjustments When the outline is complete, hit the Preview button. There may be gaps or rough edges around your subject, so use the Edge Touchup tool to shave layers of pixels from the edges.

Why the Extract filter?

The pros and cons of the tool

The Extract filter is found at the top of the Filter menu, and separates itself from other Selection tools, as it uses its own window. When loaded up, inside the filter you'll notice a number of adjustments and tools specific to the filter. An advantage to using the Extract method is that you paint over the edges of your subject, and the level of precision is adjusted with the brush size. There are touch-up tools too, and an Eraser tool to smarten up your selection. A disadvantage, however, is that the process of selection is very slow on whatever the subject is. We recommend using the filter for picking out small items in your image for a quick and accurate extraction.

Working non-destructively

How to overcome this destructive

The Extract filter works by taking a subject out of one layer and removing the remaining image. This means that when you've created your mask in the filter's window and hit OK, your image is permanently affected by the filter. The way to get around this snag is to create a duplicate of the layer you wish to work on before going into the filter. Drag the layer onto the Create New Layer button at the bottom of the Layers palette, and then head to Filter>Extract to begin the selection on this duplicate layer. The original image is kept in a perfect state underneath.

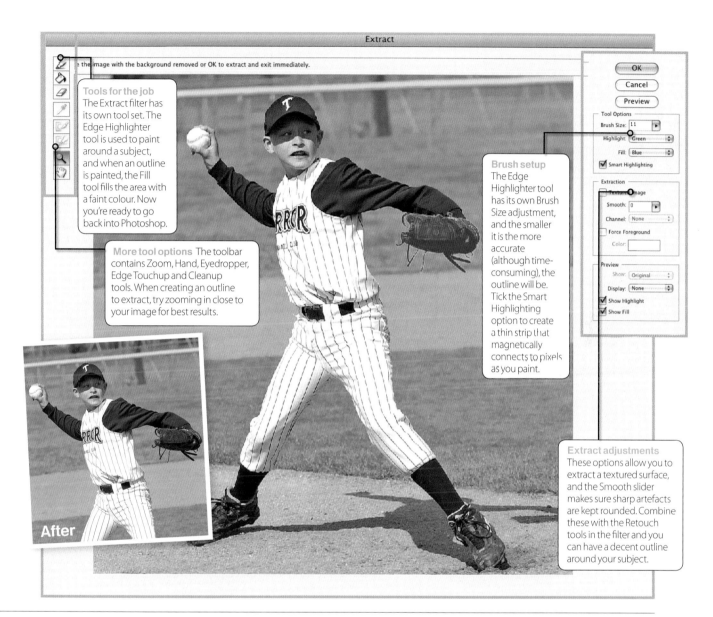

Extract

the image with the background removed or OK to extract and exit immediately.

Tools for the job
The Extract filter has its own tool set. The Edge Highlighter tool is used to paint around a subject, and when an outline is painted, the Fill tool fills the area with a faint colour. Now you're ready to go back into Photoshop.

More tool options The toolbar contains Zoom, Hand, Eyedropper, Edge Touchup and Cleanup tools. When creating an outline to extract, try zooming in close to your image for best results.

Brush setup
The Edge Highlighter tool has its own Brush Size adjustment, and the smaller it is the more accurate (although time-consuming), the outline will be. Tick the Smart Highlighting option to create a thin strip that magnetically connects to pixels as you paint.

After

Extract adjustments
These options allow you to extract a textured surface, and the Smooth slider makes sure sharp artefacts are kept rounded. Combine these with the Retouch tools in the filter and you can have a decent outline around your subject.

In newer versions of PS
Where to find this for CS4 and CS5

If you're a CS3 or earlier user of PS, you can benefit from the Extract filter appearing at the top of the Filter menu. If you're using versions CS4 or CS5, the filter has been removed from the menu and planted online at the Photoshop Updates section on **www.adobe.com/downloads/updates**. Mac users with CS5 will have to go without the Extract filter unfortunately, but we can recommend the Refine Edge command to be a worthy replacement. Once downloaded, install the filter into your Photoshop plug-ins folder and it should appear in the Filter menu after a quick restart.

Precision selections
Time-consuming yet worth it

The Extract filter can be applied to a very accurate degree using the Smart Highlighting command. In the filter's window, under Tool Options, make certain the Smart Highlighting box is ticked before painting around the edges of your subject. This ensures the brush is pixel-sensitive, similar to that of the Magnetic Lasso tool. Zoom in close to your image to make an accurate selection to extract. This process will take much longer though, so it's worth doing on smaller objects.

Fix chromatic aberration

Have your images been cursed by colour fringing? Here's a quick way to sort it out in minutes

Even with high-quality cameras, we can still fall victim to annoying problems that blight our images. Chromatic aberration is one such problem, where the lens fails to adequately capture all the colours in a scene, causing a weird fringe effect between dark and light areas. As with our example here, it is often seen in landscapes, especially around trees or plants that are against the sky. Photoshop does have a dedicated tool for fixing this found in the Lens Correction filter, but we have an easier way.

Top tip: Instead of using Hue/Saturation to desaturate the fringe colour, use it to introduce a different colour. Maybe use a light green to liven up an otherwise dark tree.

Before

After

QUICK FIX

FIX FRINGING WITH HUE/SATURATION
Select the annoying areas and suck out the colour

01 Zoom in to isolate Open your image in Photoshop. Press Cmd/Ctrl and the '+' key to zoom in to an area with fringing. In our case it is on the leaves.

02 Select the fringing Scoot up to the Select menu and pick Color Range. Use the eyedropper to click on a purple fringe area and then move the Fuzziness slider to target all incidences of the colour. Press OK. If you haven't got the Color Range feature, use the Magic Wand tool.

03 Reduce the fringe Go to Image>Adjustments>Hue/Saturation and move the Saturation slider to the left. This will strip out all of the fringing colour.

Selectively boost colour in images

QUICK FIX

Control the colours of each subject to add or reduce their saturation

The difficulty of making a specific selection is one of the reasons you might avoid the correction of colour. Ever thought 'I wish that sky was bluer' or 'if only those red bricks had a better tone'? Well, using a Hue/Saturation adjustment layer along with its eyedroppers, boosting colour requires no selections whatsoever! It's as simple as deciding which one needs changing, picking them out from the rest and then adjusting a slider.

Top tip: There's nothing stopping you from using more than one Hue/Saturation adjustment layer to adapt more than one colour in your image – just use the eyedropper to pick it out each time.

Before

After

ENHANCE YOUR HUES
Pick your colour and make it pop

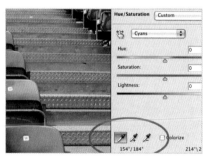

01 **Assess colours** With your image open, add a Hue/Saturation adjustment layer from the menu via Layer>New Adjustment Layer. Decide which colour is in need of a boost of saturation and then select it from the drop-down list (default is set to Master). For this image we went for Cyan to adjust the seats.

02 **Get selective** In the Hue/Saturation adjustment menu there are three eyedroppers. Use the first to click on the colour you want to boost. This will move the markers on the colourful bar to a range of tones for the subject. You can also make sure a tone isn't affected by using the other two eyedroppers to add or subtract colours.

03 **Boost colour** Once the eyedroppers have been used to pick out the colours, use the Saturation slider to either boost or reduce the amount of colour. We boosted the Saturation of these seats to +50 to make them stand out more. The sky also increased in blueness too, which complements the overall effect.

TOOL TRICKS

The Patch tool

Image repair has never been easier, thanks to this great tool

The Patch tool is incredibly easy to use, and is perfect for restoring and repairing any parts of your photos that are damaged or blemished.

This tool is a Photoshop staple, and has been around since version 6.0 of our favourite app. It's the ideal option for quick image edits, as it enables you to replace large or small selections from your images with equally large or small portions of replacement image information.

The Patch tool is tucked away in the toolbar, sharing space with the Healing brush, and can be accessed by holding the cursor down on the small black arrow and activating the fly-out menu. Once the tool is selected, three options are added to the top menu bar: Source, Destination and Use Pattern.

There are a few methods available to repair your images using the Patch tool. First, you can choose to select the 'bad' part of your image and move this selection around the photo to find an acceptable portion to put in its place. Alternatively, you can select a good part of your image first, and then move this to cover or 'patch' the unsightly part. Finally, if you don't have enough image to patch up the problem area, you can opt to patch the problem spot with a pattern fill, combining the texture of your pattern with the underlying colours present in your photograph.

Patch it up

Here's a quick and easy guide to using the Patch tool. This is a very speedy way to cover up those lumps, bumps, creases and blemishes in one swoop…

01 Getting ready
Open your start image and activate the Patch tool by pressing the letter 'J'. You can also find it in the toolbar along with the Healing brush. Notice the options that appear in the top toolbar.

02 Select a source
Your source point is the area that needs fixing. Pick the Source option in the top toolbar and select the area just as you would when using the Lasso, ie plot a selection around your object.

03 Drag 'n drop
When the selection is complete, place the cursor in the centre of the selection. Now drag it to another area of your image that can be used to patch up the blemish, then release.

Patch the bad bits
Select, drag and click

The walkthrough above shows how to patch an image by dragging the selected blemish to a clean part of the picture. You can also do the opposite, and select a clean part of your image first, then drag this over the blemish. To put this into practice, simply select the Patch tool as usual, then hit Destination instead of Source. Now you can select a fresh, clean image part, place your cursor in the centre of the selection and drag the patch over the blemish mark. Your picture will be as good as new!

Patchwork patterns
Another repair fix

Sometimes your image may have areas of foliage or texture that simply need a bit of smoothing over, as opposed to specific patching up. In this instance, choose the Patch tool as usual and opt for Source. Make a selection around your trouble-spot, then go to the top toolbar and click the blue drop-down menu next to the Use Pattern tab. Select an appropriate pattern to apply to your image, and hit Use Pattern when done. You'll see your image patched with your chosen pattern. This is ideal for areas of your designs that simply need texture.

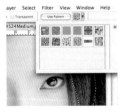

Source or Destination? When using the Patch tool, choose Source when selecting your problem areas and Destination when selecting a clean image to patch over the bad.

Colour your mask If the colour of your mask is too similar to the colours within your image, double-click on the Quick Mask icon. Now click on the Color swatch and select a colour. You can adjust the opacity here as well.

Patch tool This tool shares the same well as the Healing brush on the toolbar. To access the tool, just hold down the cursor over the small black arrow and the fly-out menu will appear.

Smudge tool For a quick touch-up to the seams of your patchwork, try opting for something like the Smudge tool to help soften the edges.

Making selections
The alternative option

The Patch tool automatically assigns you with a Selection tool. This behaves exactly like the Lasso tool in operation, but is not always the most accurate way to cut out unsightly objects; there are times when the Marquee, Magic Wand or another Selection tool will be more beneficial. Luckily, however, there is another option. You can also make a selection with your favourite Selection tool first and then activate the Patch tool afterwards. This is a more controlled way of doing things.

The finishing touch
Disguise all patchwork

We have to admit that despite its great performance, the Patch tool is in no way a miracle remedy. In most cases there will be some additional fix that needs to be done to help blend in the joins. One of the easiest ways to do this is to select the Smudge tool (R) from the toolbar and turn the Strength down on the top toolbar to around 20%. Now gently work at the edges of your new patch, and then watch it blend into the surface of your image.

Before

Different tools for different subjects

Depending on what type of subject you're dealing with, different Selection tools will have to be used. For this tutorial we used the Pen tool to make the selection because the doll had rounded edges. On more complex subjects, with many tricky areas to select, try using the Magic Wand tool to get to those extra-small pixels. Or see how effective the Magnetic Lasso tool is, as this will hug onto similar-looking pixels in one area.

Spotless backgrounds

Save hours of studio time and use Photoshop to make clean, pure white backgrounds

Cleaning up messy backgrounds is an important technique for any photographer to master. Whether behind the camera or using Photoshop, it's vital to keep a white background entirely white.

It's a lot quicker to clean up backgrounds using Photoshop rather than adjusting multiple studio lights to minimise irritating shadows. In this tutorial, you'll learn exactly how to do it. With the tools and techniques we've used here, tidying things up doesn't need to be a lengthy process.

In the following steps you'll discover how to use the Pen tool to make new selections around a subject to eventually cut them out, plus how to add a new layer mask to make the whole effect work. Tweaking adjustments such as Levels is also covered to make sure the subject will

look balanced with the white background that you'll eventually have. The best bit of this technique is that we're going to achieve all of this in just eight steps, meaning that it only takes a matter of minutes to get a good result.

So it doesn't matter if you have a black background or just a very dirty-looking one that needs whitening. It can all be sorted within a handful of steps, and won't take you long. It doesn't have to stop there, because you can also change the colour of the background to anything you want – depending on how you intend to use it.

Before we begin, you will need to find a suitable image to start work on. If you don't have one to hand, snap a household object against a roughly white background and use that.

SMARTEN UP YOUR BACKGROUND USING A LAYER MASK
Make a selection and say goodbye to the grey areas

01 Select the Pen tool Open the image that you want to work on. Make the image editable by double-clicking its layer in the Layers palette. Select the doll's shadow with the Lasso, go to Image>Adjustments>Hue/Saturation and reduce Saturation to -40. Now choose the Pen tool to draw an outline around the doll.

02 Draw the outline With the Pen tool selected and zoomed in closely, begin marking the points around the edges of the doll, adjusting the lines to fit its curves. Try to be as accurate as possible, so the final result will have seamless edges.

03 Make Selection When you've completed the whole doll, Ctrl/right-click inside the selection and hit Make Selection. This will transform the line into a live selection, making it a new Alpha channel in the Channels palette. If at any point the selection disappears, simple hold Cmd/Ctrl and click on the Alpha channel's layer to restore the selection.

04 Create a new layer In the Layers palette select the Create New Layer button at the bottom of the palette. Now drag the new layer, while inside the Layers palette, so that it sits below the layer with the doll. This new layer will form the spotless white background that we need.

05 Make grey into white With the new layer selected, hit Cmd/Ctrl+D to deselect the live selection around the doll. Go to Edit>Fill, and in the Fill menu set Contents to White, Normal for the blend mode, and use 100% Opacity. Press OK and the new layer will fill with pure white.

06 White before your eyes Go back into the Channels palette, and while holding Cmd/Ctrl click on the Alpha channel. The selection made earlier will now become visible around the doll. Go to the Layers palette, select the Doll layer and hit Add Layer Mask. This will hide the grey and show the white layer underneath.

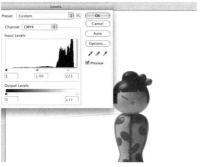

07 Levels adjustment Select the thumbnail of the doll in the Layers palette. It's the perfect time to brighten it up, so head to Image>Adjustments>Levels and boost the highlights and midtones levels of the doll. Hit OK when done.

08 Reveal the shadow The finishing touch is to add the shadow. To do this, select the Layer Mask thumbnail in the Layers palette and use a soft brush to take away the area of the mask covering the shadow. The doll should now be on a perfect white background.

Tips & fixes

Adjustment layers

You can tweak your photo with adjustment layers. Just click on the black and white icon at the foot of the Layers palette and choose from multiple editing options such as Levels and Curves.

Finer details

To really get a clean look, make sure you zoom in close to parts of your image when painting onto your mask. If you make a mistake and reveal too much of the image underneath, simply switch to white and paint the smoothness back in. Altering the size of your brush will help you get into the finer areas of the image.

Before retouch

Create flawless skin

Give portraits a quick and easy makeover using masks

We all want flawless skin, but in photographs our complexions can often look blotchy, red and patchy. Thankfully, Photoshop has just the tools to help us rescue any such skin scenarios, without the need for an intensive facial.

In this tutorial you'll learn how to create a smooth and even skintone, while maintaining facial details such as the eyes and lips. The technique is very simple and can be applied to virtually any portrait image. You will make extensive use of the Noise filter to achieve a smooth base layer for

the skin. We will then follow this up by applying a layer mask and using a brush to paint finer details back in.

By altering the opacity of our brush we can also give more form back to the face, reintroducing highlights and shape, for a natural feel.

If you are unfamiliar with masks, this is a fantastic introduction to the feature, providing a sense of just what it's capable of. You will learn how to apply a mask and use the brush to hide and reveal parts of the image with the mask. You can use any portrait image that you like to give this tutorial a go for yourself.

MAKE EVERYTHING SMOOTH, THEN WORK BACKWARDS
Apply a filter and mask to the bits you want to reveal

01 Set up Open your image, then go to Image>Mode>CMYK. Drag the background layer onto the New Layer tab to create a copy. With the background copy layer selected, go to Filter>Noise> Dust & Scratches. Set Threshold to 0 and Radius to 6px. Hit OK.

02 Mask Click the Add Layer Mask icon at the foot of the Layers palette. Pick a big black brush and paint over the hair, background and clothing. Painting with black will reveal the sharpness below. Click the eye icon off the background layer to see the mask.

03 Smaller details Next, select a smaller brush (or hit the '[' key) and use this to carefully paint over the eyes and lips. Ensure you are still using black to paint with. You will now see the detail return to these areas.

04 Add detail The skin now looks a bit too smooth, so to add some realism pick a medium-size soft brush set to black, and lower the brush Opacity to 25% in the top Options bar. Sweep the brush over the main facial features, following the contours of the nose, eyebrows, chin, neck and cleavage.

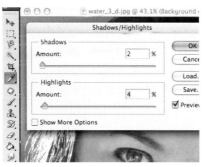

05 Add some warmth To add some warmth to this photo, go to Image> Adjustments>Shadow/Highlights and enter 2% for Shadows and 4% for Highlights. Hit OK. You'll need to experiment with these amounts if you are using your own photo.

06 A little more refinement Now go to the Layers palette and reduce Fill to between 70% and 80%. This will give the skin a bit more texture without losing all the smoothness.

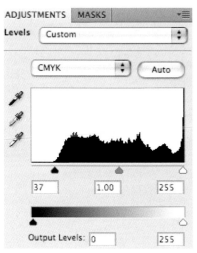

07 Level it out These final two steps are optional. To add a bit more punch to the image go to the Adjustment Layer icon at the bottom of the Layers palette. Pull the black slider inwards until it's in line with the start of the histogram information. Do the same with the white slider if you need to.

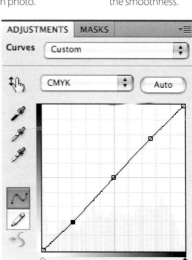

08 Curves Now add another adjustment layer and this time select Curves. Click on the top portion of the line (about a third of the way down) and pull it upwards just a little. Now click on the bottom third of the line and pull downwards a little. It creates a slight S-shaped curve to help boost contrast without clipping highlights or losing detail in the shadows.

Remove red-eye

Cure the curse of red-eye in your portrait photos with the Red Eye Removal tool in Photoshop

The effect known as red-eye is caused by light hitting the blood vessels in the retina at the back of the eye and bouncing directly out to the camera. It causes the pupil to appear red rather than black and happens when a flash is used that is situated very close to the lens itself. With Photoshop's Red Eye tool you can fix this remarkably quickly and easily as it is designed to work almost automatically.

Before

QUICK FIX
After

Top tip: Don't attempt to draw the Red Eye Removal box so that it covers just the pupil. Draw it large enough to encompass the pupil and iris so the tool has enough area to work on.

PERFECT YOUR PORTRAIT
Eliminate this common photographic problem

01 **Load and zoom** Load the image with the problem and zoom in to the left eye. This may be around 300% depending on the file size. Duplicate the Background layer in the Layers palette so it can be scrapped if you need to revert back to the original.

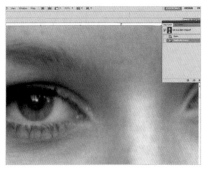

02 **Use the tool** The Red Eye Removal tool is in the same group as the Healing Brush. Draw a large box covering the pupil and iris. With the default settings it should remove all the red and not leak outside the pupil. Repeat the process on the other eye and merge the layers when you're done.

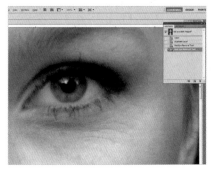

03 **The options** If the eye still looks slightly red, undo the action then increase the Darken amount from 50% to 80% and try again. If the effect hasn't covered all the red area then increase the Pupil Size. If there's some black bleeding into the iris, reduce the Pupil Size.

Control Unsharp Mask

Squeeze a bit more from Unsharp Mask with the Fade option

QUICK FIX

It is so easy to get caught up in controlling all the options available in an edit that you forget that it's possible to edit the edit! The Fade command is a useful tool that allows you to reduce the intensity of an edit but still keep the essence of what you want to do.

One of the best ways to see this in action is to use it with the Unsharp Mask filter. We all know how handy this is in sharpening up images, but we also all know that it can be a tightrope between getting the sharpness needed and ending up with loads of 'halos'. With the Fade command, however, you can ramp up Unsharp Mask and then get rid of the halos later. Hoorah!

Top tip: The Fade command is available for a lot of tools and is always worth trying if your edit doesn't look quite right. It's much better than starting again...

Before

After

BE A MASTER OF UNSHARP MASK
Don't let the halos ruin your edit!

01 **Apply the filter** Open up the image you want to edit and then go up to the Filter menu. Go down to Sharpen and then across to Unsharp Mask.

02 **Make the edit** Usually Unsharp Mask involves a dance between getting the sharpness you want and avoiding any halos. Don't worry this time – use the sliders to sharpen up your edges without fear of recrimination. Click OK when done.

03 **Bring it back** Go up to the Edit menu and pick Fade Unsharp Mask (this obviously changes if you have used a different tool). Now use the Opacity slider to bring back the halos but still keep the sharpness! You can try different blending modes for an extra finish.

Tips & fixes

Painting with the Color Replacement tool

The tool works on the basis that you keep the crosshair on the colour at all times when painting. On an edge that's against a similar colour, reduce the Tolerance value to 10% or lower. It's a case of playing with the Tolerance value for an accurate replacement.

Use the Color Replacement tool

Discover the creative possibilities of this hidden wonder

The extent of Photoshop's ability doesn't stop on the surface of what's there when you load it up. The toolbar actually contains many more tools than are visible, with sometimes two, three, four or more options than you first see.

The Color Replacement tool is one of these – hidden in the Brushes group (shortcut 'B') because it performs in the same way as the Brush tool but with mannerisms of the Selection tools. This tool is used by taking a colour and painting over a subject to swap two colours. It's similar to the Color Balance and Hue adjustments (Image menu), but you choose the colour that you want to use. After the first spot of paint is applied, the tool cleverly ignores all other colours and only changes that particular one.

The best aspect of this tool is that it retains the lighting on the subject that you're colour swapping. This means that highlights and shadows are preserved in your image. But the trick is to make sure the chosen colour for the replacement has the right brightness for the effect to look most natural. Otherwise you could end up with a blotchy outcome. The Tolerance value is the most important aspect of the Color Replacement tool, because it controls how much paint is applied.

Follow our quick and easy tutorial on using the Color Replacement tool to give this bowl of fruit a funky makeover in minutes. You can try it out with your own picture and start practising your colour replacement skills!

THE BEST OF THE BUNCH
Use the Color Replacement tool to swap colours around

01 **Set up the brush** Open up your start image and then Duplicate the layer so you have a copy with the original colours and select the Color Replacement tool. In the Options bar set Mode to Color, Sampling to Once, Limit to Contiguous, Tolerance to 100%, Size to 200px.

02 **Test colours** Open the Foreground Color picker, choose a colour, or one from a fruit, and use the tool to paint a small patch on one of the fruits. If it's too dark/light it looks blocky. When happy, in the Color picker hit Add To Swatches. Repeat for each colour on all the fruit, saving each colour as a new swatch.

03 **Red bananas!** Go to Window> Swatches to open the saved colours. For the bananas we chose red from one of the strawberries – but click on the swatch you saved for the bananas. Paint close to the edges using the Color Replacement tool, but make sure you don't go over them.

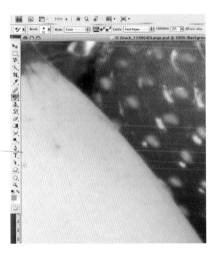

04 **Edges** Before we replace colours of the other fruits, touch up the banana edges. In the Options bar change the settings to Sampling Continuous, Limits to Find Edges, Tolerance to 20%. Lower the tool's Hardness to 0%. Zoom to 300% and paint to the edges. Don't worry if it's rough, we'll tidy up later.

05 **Orange apple** In the Swatches palette click on the colour you saved for the apple. As with the bananas, use a Brush Size of 200px and the settings in step 1 to paint the apple, leaving a thin strip of green around the edges.

06 **Finer details** Zoom in to 300% and set the Options bar for painting the edges as we did with the bananas. Make the colour replacement around the edge of the apple and around the stalk. We'll correct imperfections later on.

07 **Last but not least** For the oranges, choose the colour you saved as a swatch to paint over the fruit. We chose the green of the apple. Paint each orange to the edges using the settings Sampling: Continuous, Limits: Find Edges and Tolerance 20%.

08 **Tidy the layer mask** On the layer with replacing colours click on the Add Layer Mask button in the Layers palette. Zoom in to 300% and use the Brush tool on the white layer mask thumbnail to erase any rough edges around each of the pieces of fruit.

Before

After

Before

After

Fail-safe photo fixes

Get to grips with three fail-safe techniques for improving landscape imagery and two more for portraits. They are a great way of improving images

We've got five different fail-safe techniques for you here demonstrated on two very different images: the first a landscape and the second a portrait. You'll find out how a simple Shadow/Highlight adjustment can transform a landscape image by throwing light into the shadows, with one very pleasant spin-off: a wonderful shift in colour and saturation.

It works best on photographs with natural shadow areas, meaning some degree of

sunshine is needed. You won't get the same results with an image captured on an overcast day. The technique that follows can similarly be applied to any landscape scene, as long as it has visible sky. Darken it down with a Curves adjustment to increase impact, and apply a gradient to maintain a realistic feel.

Last but not least on the landscape front we have a trick to reduce the impact of camera shake, courtesy of the Smart Sharpen filter. It doesn't work miracles but it can make significant improvements.

On the portrait front you'll learn how to set up contrast to ensure a full contrast range, from the darkest dark to the lightest light. It's not portrait specific and can be applied to any image. It's applied by Levels and is all about setting up the end points without clipping shadow or highlight detail. The final technique teaches you how to give a skin a wonderfully warm glow with a targeted Saturation adjustment. It will work on all colours of skin tone and you can tweak the Saturation sliders to suit.

IMPROVE AN IMAGE WITH SHADOW/HIGHLIGHT WORK
Throwing light into shadows can transform a dull-looking shot

01 Duplicate background layer The blacks look very heavy in this image, and distract from the rest of the scene. The first thing we're going to do is to throw a little detail into the darker areas. Duplicate the background layer with Cmd/Ctrl+ J.

02 Test the sliders We work the sliders to see what effect they each have on our tones. It appears that Tonal Width is most useful to our image as we have a wide range of shadow tones that need brightening, so we use a high setting of 100% to lighten shadows as much as possible.

03 Complete the work The Amount then controls the overall strength of the Tonal Width work while the Radius controls how far out from a single pixel the calculations for brightening are applied. Low settings can make things look too soft or make halos look apparent. We settle on settings of 100 for all three for a bright, hyper-real feel.

GIVE SKIES A MORE DRAMATIC FEEL
This technique can be applied to skies of any kind

04 Select Gradient tool Now we can work on the sky with a little bit of gradient-based burning (darkening). Add a Curves adjustment layer using the button at the bottom of the Layers palette. Now select the Gradient tool (under the Paintbucket tool if not visible in the Tools palette) and select the first of five icons in the tool Options bar.

05 Set up the tool Click the Gradient Picker (drop down menu in the Tool Options Bar) and make sure Foreground to Background is selected; it's the first preset top left. OK the dialog and press 'D' to reset your colour palette to white and black.

06 Draw the gradient Now drop the Curves adjustment down with a single point to darken. The image will darken as a whole. To focus this on the sky instead, draw a straight vertical line with the Gradient tool from halfway down the sky to the horizon, making sure the Curves layer mask is still active.

07 Boost sky colour We can increase Saturation in the sky too. Cmd/Ctrl-click the layer mask on the Curves layer to load it as a selection, then add a Hue/Saturation adjustment layer using the Layers palette button as previous. Push Saturation up to +30.

08 Change sky colour We can use the same adjustment to alter the colour of the sky if we like, via the Hue slider. A shift to -5 gives the sky a more turquoise hue. To prevent either of these adjustments further affecting the brightness of the sky, change its layer blending mode from Normal to Color.

Fix motion blur

This image was shot at 1/60sec shutter speed which with a hefty zoom lens makes camera shake a problem. A quick zoom in shows a touch of movement blur so let's look at improving sharpness.

01 100% zoom It's important to zoom in to 100% or Actual Pixels to check sharpness. A good keyboard shortcut is Cmd/Ctrl+Opt/Alt+0

02 Move around image Hold down Space and click and drag to move around the image to check if the blur is a focus or camera shake issue.

03 Duplicate layer There's movement blur here. To remove it, first duplicate your working layer with Cmd/Ctrl+J to preserve the original info.

04 Smart Sharpen filter Go to Filter>Sharpen> Smart Sharpen. In the Remove box select Motion Blur. Start with 100% Amount and 1.0 pixel Radius.

05 Test and apply Now simply move the Angle dial around until you reach the best-looking result. Increase Radius and Amount to suit you taste.

IMPROVE THE CONTRAST OF ANY IMAGE WITH A LEVELS ADJUSTMENT Use the exposure clipping display to guarantee optimum contrast

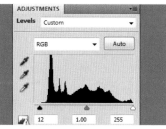

09 **Add Levels layer** If your aim is to produce a final image with good contrast, the first step is to check the endpoints with a Levels adjustment. Add the Levels layer using the button at the Layers palette base. Check to see if the information reaches both ends of the histogram.

10 **Analyse the histogram** On the right-hand side (highlights) you can see that the information reaches the end, so no need for correction. On the left-hand side (shadows) there's a gap, so we can improve contrast here. Hold down Opt/Alt, click the black slider and start to drag it inwards.

11 **Set up shadow tones** You'll see a blank white screen. As you move inwards, some coloured or black information will appear. Move back until the information just disappears off screen. Release the mouse and your contrast work is done. You can repeat the method for highlights if it's necessary.

GIVE SKIN A HEALTHY GLOW WITH FOCUSED SATURATION WORK
Working specific colour ranges produces better results

12 **Add Hue/ Saturation layer** You can give a healthy glow to skin tones by increasing saturation of the Red and Yellow tones, the main constituents of all skin types. Start by adding a Hue/Saturation adjustment layer using the button at the bottom of the Layers palette

13 **Focus the adjustment** Now select Reds from the drop-down menu that says Master by default. Push Saturation up to about +25. Now do the same with Yellows. This will also add a bit more colour to the hair.

14 **Mask out the foliage** Green foliage has a high yellow constituent so the background looks saturated. We can brush the adjustment out using the layer mask. Take a soft-edge black brush, and with the layer mask active, simply brush over the foliage.

15 **Change blending mode** Saturation adjustments can alter the Luminosity (brightness) of the image. As we don't want the image brightened or darkened, we prevent this by changing the blending mode from Normal to Saturation. This will protect the luminosity.

Add emphasis to eyes

Use Dodge and Burn to give the eyes a sparkle

It's well known that a person's eyes are the windows to their soul. Here's a very quick way to draw more attention to them in a portrait image.

To add more punch to the eyes, we've used two tools for the job: the Burn tool and the Dodge tool. The first of these is great for deepening shadows, which in turn makes the highlights stand out. But to really create a polished effect, the Dodge tool is the perfect way to add that all-important sparkle.

Give it a go – it only takes five minutes and works on any photo.

Top tip: For an extra boost, use the Burn tool and a small brush to darken the eyelashes along the top and bottom.

QUICK FIX

After

Before

USE THE DODGE AND BURN TOOLS
Add contrast to eyes in three quick steps

01 **Non-destructive editing** To edit non-destructively on your image, drag the image's layer onto the Create New Layer button in the Layers palette to duplicate. This way you can return to the original image at any point while editing.

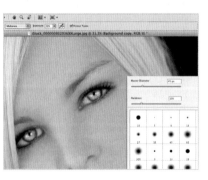

02 **Lighten** Pick the Dodge tool and set its brush size so that the tip covers the coloured area of the iris. Set the tool's Hardness to 20%, and in the Options bar change Range to Midtones, Exposure to 30%, and tick the Protect Tones box. Softly paint over the iris to add contrast and brightness.

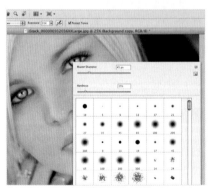

03 **Darken the edges** Select the Burn tool and set it to 15% Hardness with a brush size that fits over the outline of the iris. Set the Range to Shadows and Exposure to 15%. Apply the brush to the outside edge of the iris, making the area darker.

Edit with gradients

Put some sparkle into dull images using gradients

Gradients are often used in the realm of digital design, but rarely do they come into play for photo edits.

They can actually be extremely useful, especially when teamed with blending modes. In our example here, we have a photo taken on a dull day. The sky is grey and the foreground looks underexposed. By applying a gradient, though, it's possible to add colour to the sky and also deal with the exposure problem. And it all starts with a simple selection. Give it a go on one of your own images.

Top tip: Experiment with different gradient colours to emulate the look of traditional lens filters.

QUICK FIX

Before

After

FIX DULL SKIES AND POOR EXPOSURE
Three steps to culling the dull

01 **Make a selection** First up, isolate the sky. Use the Magic Wand if there is lots of contrast. Once selected, create a new layer and then click on the Gradient tool. Make sure you have Linear Gradient selected and then click the Gradient bar to open the Gradient Editor.

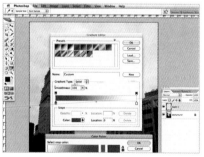

02 **Pick your hue** Click the Black, White gradient from the Presets panel then click the black Color Stop below the gradient bar. Click the Color bar at the bottom left and then select a dark blue. Click OK to return to your canvas and hold down Shift on the keyboard to drag the cursor from the top to the bottom. Fill the sky area with blue.

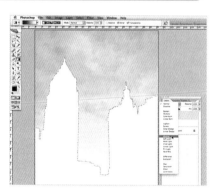

03 **Blend to edit** To let the gradient colour merge with the photo, pick the Overlay blending mode. Now create a new layer, go to Select>Inverse and then Edit>Fill and pick White. Apply the Overlay blending mode again and the dull foreground will zing!

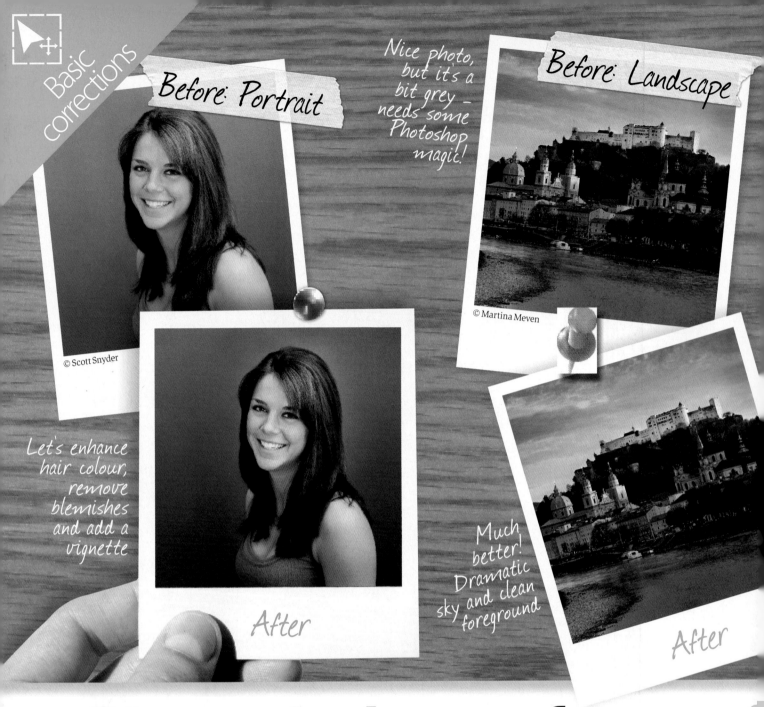

Basic corrections

Before: Portrait

© Scott Snyder

Nice photo, but it's a bit grey – needs some Photoshop magic!

Before: Landscape

© Martina Meven

Let's enhance hair colour, remove blemishes and add a vignette

After

Much better! Dramatic sky and clean foreground

After

Six techniques for pe

Transform any photograph from average to brilliant, with these six simpl

It's a good idea to compare Photoshop to cooking, because you can follow a recipe in each to get what you want – but when using Photoshop, as with cooking, it's at its best when you (the 'cook') deviate from the recipe and learn how to put your own spin on things.

So think of these techniques as ingredients and this article as the recipe. Read it, learn it and then play with it until you have your own version of 'Six techniques for perfect pictures' that suit your own taste. You can try all of these skills out on your own photos, so gather together a portrait, a landscape and a macro to work on.

Our first technique involves a retouching layer – and this is what you should always start with for any given image. Using the Cloning tools directly on the image is destructive to the pixels, so by creating a blank layer and setting up your tools correctly you are able to work non-destructively.

We're going to use adjustment layers for the next three techniques, starting with Curves for density, because no matter how good a photographer you are, the exposure of the image will always need to be adjusted. After that's completed, you'll be adding some ambience using a solid colour.

Before: Macro

This macro image is crying out for some enhancement

© Sisi Fili

It's amazing what a bit of colour work and sharpening can do!

After

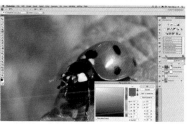

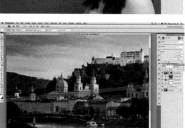

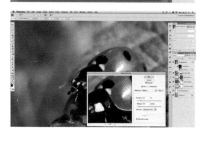

Each technique explained

Sometimes in digital photography you need to get back to basics, with non-destructive editing the order of the day. Let us introduce you to six essential techniques that will help you get perfect pictures every time you open Photoshop

01 Retouching layer The retouching layer works in partnership with the Clone Stamp tool and the Healing brush as a protective barrier.

02 Density curves A Curves adjustment layer is all that you need to subtly improve the density of the image.

03 Colour mood Adjusting colour is not always about correction. You can use a Solid Color adjustment layer to add warmth and atmosphere.

04 Colour focus We can use colour for focus and draw the viewer's attention towards the point of interest with a little saturation.

05 Vignetting Vignetting is a technique that's as old as photography, and it's used to lighten the point of interest into focus.

06 Smart sharpening Whether shooting JPEG or RAW, every image needs sharpening at the end of the day. So why not do this non-destructively?

ect pics

nage-editing methods

Two techniques commonly employed to draw emphasis towards the point of focus in a shot are colour saturation and darkening of the corners, and this is precisely what you're going to be doing next as you selectively apply more saturation to your subject and points of interest, because colour attracts the eye.

You'll then copy all the pixels into a new inter-merge layer and use that to darken or vignette the area surrounding your subject, so that it becomes slightly lighter and a little more interesting.

Finally, where would we be without some Smart sharpening on a Smart filter for a crisp finish!

Essential technique 1: *The retouching layer*

Creating a blank layer is such a simple thing to do in Photoshop, yet it opens up a host of possibilities for not only working non-destructively, but also giving yourself the chance to remove any errors subtly with the Eraser tool without affecting any of the cloning or healing that you've already done. In the case of a landscape image it gives you the chance to remove unwanted elements of water, rubbish and even birds flying in the sky. Macro images can magnify all the defects of the natural world, and a retouching layer lets you tidy up any imperfections while retaining full control of all the original pixels. But it's on a portrait image that a retouching layer really shines, because you can remove stray hairs, refine skin details and banish unwanted wrinkles, all on a separate layer.

Apply the technique

After

Before

Landscapes need to be clean, and the retouch layer is perfect for removing birds, rubbish and unwanted items

01 **New layer** Create a new layer by clicking on the New Layer icon in the Layers panel. It's probably one of the simplest tasks you'll ever complete within Photoshop, but its power is not to be underestimated when used with the Tools panel.

02 **Renaming layer** Double-click on the (Layer 1) text in the new layer to activate it and then rename it ('Retouching layer'). Renaming layers keeps you organised and makes finding things much easier.

03 **Layer mask** Click the Layer Mask icon in the Layers panel to add a default Reveal All layer mask. This stage is essential for portraits but optional for other genres. In CS4 or CS5 add layer masks via the Masks panel.

04 **Set up the Healing brush** Press 'J' for the Healing brush or Shift+J to cycle through the Healing tools. Once the tool is active, choose All Layers from the Sample menu in the Options bar.

05 **Use the Healing brush** Click on your retouch layer to activate it, then hold down Opt/Alt to sample the part of the image you wish to use as the texture. Now click and drag your mouse or graphics pen over the area you wish to heal.

06 **Set up the Clone tool** Press 'S' for the Clone Stamp, or Shift+S to cycle through the tools. Once the tool is active, choose All Layers from the Sample menu and set the Opacity to 75% in the Options bar at the top.

07 **Use the Clone tool** This tool works in the same fashion as the Healing brush. What you will have to do, depending on the image and subject, is work between the tools – all the time making sure the cloned pixels are placed on the retouch layer.

Essential technique 2: *Density curves*

After

Before

The Density curve makes a subtle change by darkening the ladybird's red and black shell and the background

After

Before

In the portrait, the Density curve darkens the hair, giving it a richer feel compared to the original image

"Just be careful when brightening any shadows with curves that you don't bring out any hidden digital noise"

Highlight detail

When you adjust your image's density or exposure, you need to make sure you don't blow out the brightest parts of the image to white and lose detail in the highlights. Skies are particularly prone to loss of highlight detail, but in this particular image the side of the buildings are most at risk.

Midtone detail

The midtone detail is probably the easiest part of the image to look after, but is no less important. Make sure the colour is how it should be, and if not, you can go into the individual RGB channels and use the Color Curves to make a fine colour adjustment. When using Curves you need to keep an eye on both the shadows and highlights for any colour changes.

Tip: Use the Curves Eyedropper tool and Cmd/Ctrl-click on your image. The Brightness value will appear on the Curves line. Then just move the line up and down to lighten or darken.

Shadow detail

When you photograph a landscape, you're either going to expose for the brightest parts of the image or, depending on the scene, the darkest parts – the shadows. The two extremes of the tonal range do not like each other, and at some point compromises are going to have to be made. This is where Photoshop can help, but just be careful when brightening any shadows with curves that you don't bring out any hidden digital noise.

Essential technique 3:
Colour mood

Before

After

After

Before

Left: *Choose a slightly different shade of brown to create an evening sunset look with you own landscape images*

The Solid Color adjustment layer is blended using brown to create the warm effect of morning sun

Soft Light
When you have chosen your brown colour from the picker, you will need to blend the colour so that it interacts with the image, so go to the layer blending mode and choose Soft Light.

Brown colour
When you are picking the shade of brown for an image, with portraits you need to choose it from within the yellow spectrum, but with landscapes and nature shots you can pick a brown from the orange colour range.

Mask blurring
After revealing the brown colour throughout the hair with a soft paintbrush set to white, go to Filter> Blur>Gaussian Blur and apply 12px of blur to the mask. This will help blend the effect and hide any hard brush strokes.

Inverse mask
The quickest way to hide the Solid Color adjustment layer mask is to use the keyboard shortcut Cmd+I (Mac) or Ctrl+I (PC). This will switch the mask from the white Reveal to the black Hidden option.

Creating a colour mood layer using an adjustment layer of Solid Color is a great way to alter the colour of an image without having to resort to using any of the colour correction commands. The secret is to pick a shade of brown that works with your image. People pictures benefit from a brown selected from within the yellow colour range, whereas landscape and nature shots look better when you pick a brown from within a more orange colour range. Think of blonde hair and evening sunsets, and you won't go far wrong. Once you have selected your shade of brown, it will need to blend with your image, and the best option is to use the Soft Light blending mode, although in some cases Overlay will also work. Finally, you can use the Channel mask to reveal or hide different elements to suit your own image. When it comes to portraits, the effect is adapted to make hair look much richer and you will want to subtly reveal the effect by first of all inversing the layer mask.

> "Landscape shots look better when you pick a brown from within a more orange colour range"

Essential technique 4:
Colour focus

Before

Even though we've added a Solid Color adjustment layer to warm the evening sky, we can still use more colour, and in particular the amount of colour, or rather its saturation or vibrancy level, to attract the viewer's eye towards the different points of interest within the image.

During

In CS4+ you can click on the Vibrance adjustment layer and this will allow you to add tonally correct levels of saturation to the image. Once you have chosen the amount that looks correct hit OK. CS3 users can achieve the effect by using a Hue and Saturation adjustment layer.

After

Applying technique 4

In this technique we'll use colour saturation to focus attention on points of interest in the image. So in the case of this landscape image, the castle and building below are key areas where adding colour saturation will enhance things

01 **Adding vibrance**
Click on the Vibrance adjustment layer and adjust the vibrance amount and saturation to suit the image. In this case +15 Vibrance and +25 Saturation were adjusted for effect.

02 **Inverse layer mask**
This amount of colour saturation is too strong for an overall layer adjustment. Click the Invert Mask option to hide the effect, ready for it to be revealed subtly.

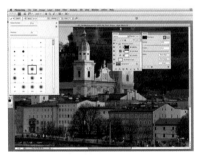

03 **Choose a brush**
Choose a Soft 65-pixel brush with Hardness set to 0. Now hit 'D' to reset your foreground and background colours, then press 'X' to rotate white to the foreground.

04 **Reveal colour**
Carefully reveal the colour saturation back on elements of the image you wish to draw the viewer's attention to, namely the most important parts – in this case the buildings.

The points of interest where you want to focus the viewer's attention will be a little more saturated than normal, and because the eye likes bright colours it will naturally be drawn to different areas of the image that are little bit more saturated, while ignoring less saturated elements.

Essential technique 5:
Vignetting

Vignetting is a technique that's as old as photography, and it's an amazing way of further drawing the viewer's attention towards elements of the image that are of interest. Traditionally, darkening occurred around the edges of an image either mechanically or optically. But we are well into the digital age, so let's opt for the pixel way of doing things. This is much more flexible, because you can offset the centre and alter the shape of the darkening to suit the image, and in the case of our three examples we used the Marquee tools to create the vignetting.

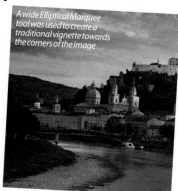

A wide Elliptical Marquee tool was used to create a traditional vignette towards the corners of the image

Before

Vignette colour

A side effect of creating a vignette is that it also saturates and alters the colour of the image. So you may have to use the Sponge tool on Desaturate at 5% Flow to calm some of the hotter colour edges down a little. You can get to the Sponge tool by pressing 'O' on the keyboard and Shift+O to cycle past the Dodge and Burn tools to reach the Sponge tool, and once you have it activated choose a soft 65px brush with 0% Hardness.

After

> "Vignetting is an amazing way of drawing the viewer's attention towards elements of the image that are of interest"

Applying the technique

01 Merge the layers Add a new blank layer and then hold down Opt/Alt and go to the Layers panel menu to select Merge Visible. The trick here is to keep holding down Opt/Alt while selecting the Merge Visible option.

02 Blending mode Rename the merged layer 'Darkening', then change the blend mode to Multiply and this will effectively double the exposure and give you the basis for the vignette effect. All you need to do now is mask the centre of the image.

When you sharpen a macro shot, you will need to pay particular attention to the areas of focus

Before

"Once the Smart sharpening has been applied, you can use the Layer Visibility icon to check the image for a before and after"

Essential technique 6:
Smart sharpening

We are going to repeat step 1 from the previous techniques, but this time hold down Shift+Alt+Ctrl+E (PC) or Shift+Opt+Cmd+E (Mac) to merge all the layers into a new composite layer. Next, navigate to Filter>Convert For Smart Filters and then Filter>Sharpen>Smart Sharpen. Select the Basic view and set Amount to 40% and Radius to 0.7 pixels. This is a really good starting point to see whether your image needs more or less sharpening. Set the Remove option to Gaussian Blur and tick the More Accurate box. Now click OK. Once the Smart sharpening has been applied, you can use the Layer Visibility icon to check the image for a before and after. Make sure you're zoomed in at 100%. If you are not, double-click the Zoom icon in order to do so. Now check the before and after with the layer visibility for the amount of sharpening used.

After

03 **Elliptical tool** Using the Elliptical Marquee tool (M), draw an elliptical selection around the centre of the image so that it covers all the important points of interest. Make sure though, that you leave enough room for the vignette to work.

04 **Add a layer mask** In the Masks panel add a layer mask by clicking the Mask icon. Now click the Invert button to make sure the vignette effect is on the outer edges and not in the centre. Using the Feather slider, increase the Amount to 120px until the vignette blends into the image.

05 **Adjust the opacity** Finally, adjust the layer opacity until you have reduced the vignette darkening down to a level where it's still darker than the middle of the image but bright enough that you get hints of detail around the edges.

Get creative

Learn how you can create art from your photos in minutes with our top tips and Photoshop's toolset

Digitally age a photo with simple Photoshop tricks

76

92

"Transform the ordinary into the extraordinary"

ESSENTIALS   DESIGN   PAINTING   »   ○ CS Live

102

Smart Objects can make your photos come to life

106

Add a frame for a stylish yet simple effect

Use the Blur filters to add a sense of motion

Imaginative portrait retouch

Creative landscape retouch

Make a vintage photograph

Creative
photo retouching

Transform the ordinary into the extraordinary and unlock your image's potential with a bit of creative retouch magic

We've got three very different subjects over the next six pages, retouched to perfection with three rather fab techniques. The first two really are testament to the fact that it pays to try and see the potential in your imagery as it first appears out of camera. Something that looks really ordinary could be a diamond in the rough. Take the case of our first portrait shot; it's

the finished image is barely recognisable as the one you started with. What your picture starts out with in terms of contrast and colour isn't even always relevant. That is the fantastic thing about postproduction after all – you have access to the entire tonal spectrum at your fingertips. So pick and choose to your heart's content! The sunset image that we take a look at next doesn't need to undergo

"The thing to remember is that while your subject isn't overly malleable without complex composite work, the colour and contrast can be revolutionised"

fairly drab and uninteresting – despite the energy in the model's face and actions – simply because the colour is washed out and the contrast is low. By picking the two dominant colours in the shot and turning them into the colour theme of the image, it's transformed into something that you simply can't look away from and becomes a real eye-catcher. The thing to remember is that while your subject isn't overly malleable without complex composite work, the colour and contrast of your image can be completely revolutionised to the point where

quite the same transformation to catch the viewer's eye, but we've still altered the colour hue to a fairly dramatic extent, albeit maintaining more reality than the portrait with its kaleidoscope sky. The final shot has a very different feel to the first two, swapping colour for sepia, and an old-worldly look. But again, if you look at the contemporary, hyper-real feel of the start image, you'd be sceptical that such a picture could be made to look like a museum piece. So take a lesson from these inspiring tutorials and see the potential in everything.

Tips & fixes

Go for contrast

We picked out colours that matched the woman's clothes, but we could have easily gone in the opposite direction and used opposite colours. Or used very subdued colours. By using the Gradient tool to apply a wash of colour over the image, you can chance the mood really easily. Experiment with different colours and see how they affect your image. It's actually a good way of learning colour theory.

Start image

Creative portrait retouch

Bring out the colours in a muted portrait and bring it to life

This combination of techniques is testament to the fact that you can transform something ordinary into something truly extraordinary with simple contrast and colour adjustments – not an ounce of compositing, painting or illustration in sight. Our subject has an energy unmatched by the original, muted colour palette so our task is to inject a contrast and tonal scheme that reflects her joie de vivre. Pink and blue are the original dominant colours so why not head right into pink and blue fantasy land with a choice bit of hair colouring and a background wash?

Quick airbrush retouch technique

Select the top layer and create a merged duplicate on top with Cmd/Ctrl+Opt/Alt+Shift+E and run a Gaussian Blur with a Radius of 10px. Add a layer mask, invert it and paint into the skin only with a soft white brush. Add 3% Gaussian Mono noise with the Add Noise filter to the layer (not the mask) to finish the effect.

TRANSFORM AN IMAGE WITH COLOUR
Pinks and blues rescue this dull portrait

01 **Set up blacks** Open up your portrait image. The blacks look too weak so we add a Levels adjustment layer. Sure enough the blacks don't reach the histogram end on the left, so we drag the black slider inwards to meet the bulk of the information at 19. The highlights are fine the other end.

02 **Boost contrast** The jeans look a little too dark, so with the layer mask still active we quickly brush out the adjustment there with a soft black brush at 100% Opacity. The image could do with a general contrast boost too, so we add a Curves adjustment layer. One point drops the shadows down a fraction and another boosts the highlights up sharply.

03 **Restore sky detail** We've lost a lot of detail in the sky by boosting the contrast, but we can rescue some of the brightest parts by Ctrl/right-clicking the Curves layer and selecting Blending Options. Hold down Opt/Alt and click the white slider on the top ramp to split it in two. Drag the left side of the slider to 225. The sky should be restored.

04 **Change the hair colour** We're going to give the hair a pink colour to match the T-shirt. Add a Color Balance adjustment layer and, with Midtones selected, change Magenta to -40 and Blue to -8. Invert the layer mask with Cmd/Ctrl+I to Hide All and carefully brush into the hair with a soft white brush, avoiding the face and shirt.

05 **Blend the hair colour** Use a brush with 50% Opacity over the fine hair to reveal part of the skin or T-shirt, and switch to black instead of white to brush the colour out of unwanted areas. Now we're ready to add to the shadow and highlight tones. Create your first Levels adjustment layer and select Blue from the drop-down menu.

06 **Add a blue tinge** Move the black output slider (bottom) to a setting of 40 to add Blue to the shadows, and then move the white input slider to 240. Select the Gradient tool, pick the Foreground to Background gradient and press 'D' on your keyboard. Draw a line from the bottom right-hand corner up to the top left. Now add another Levels adjustment layer.

07 **Pink tinge and overlays** To add pink to the highlights, set the bottom white slider to 235 for Green and the same for Blue. Drag from top right to bottom left with the Gradient tool. Now add a Solid Color adjustment layer and select a pink. Drag the gradient from top left to centre and add a sky-blue gradient in the opposite corner.

08 **Further contrast boost** Adjust the opacity on the Solid Color layers to suit and add a Curves adjustment for a final contrast boost. Plot a point in the shadows, midtones and highlights. Pull the shadows down a fraction, the midtones up strongly and the highlights up a little. See the sidebar for tips on adding even more polish!

"Colour filters have been used since year dot, to enhance the natural beauty of sunset skies"

Tips & fixes

Curves for contrast

You'll notice in Step 4, when using Curves to boost contrast, that we push the highlights up harder than we pull the shadows down. Many times an S-shaped curve is recommended for a contrast increase, but for images with a balanced array of tones across the histogram, such a shape can end up making shadows look far too dark and dense. Highlights can typically withstand more increase, so the bulk of the work should be done there, with just a small change to the shadows.

Start image

Creative landscape retouch

Transform a standard sunset scene into a spectacular blend of vivid tones with precision colour and contrast work

Colour filters have been used since year dot to enhance the natural beauty of sunset skies, so you shouldn't feel a smidgeon of guilt for offering nature a little help in transforming your sunset pics for the better. Our sunset was actually shot a little prematurely, but we can wind forward the clock with some careful exposure and contrast adjustments before tweaking the colours to produce a more fantastical result. The turquoise skies, sea and pink-orange cloud colour combination can be found in the natural world, so as spectacular as it might look, it still retains an element of reality for the critical viewing eye.

Look out for noise

When you are adjusting colour to extreme levels, always keep an eye out for noise. If you do notice that some has crept in, you can either go to the Reduce Noise filter, or you could add just the slightest amount of Gaussian Blur.

ENHANCE A SUNSET WITH COLOUR AND CONTRAST

Turn standard yellow and blue into magnificent turquoise and pink

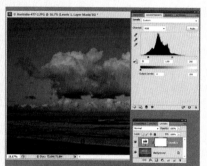

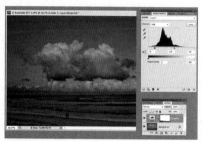

01 **Add a Levels layer** Open up your landscape image. Our shot was taken before sunset so there's still a lot of ambient light around. We want to darken the scene to produce more of a silhouette effect. Start by adding a Levels adjustment layer.

02 **Clip the blacks** Now drag the top black slider to 35. You can see we're moving past of lot of shadow information on the histogram which means we're clipping detail to pure black – necessary if we want to create an accurate silhouette finish.

03 **Restore beach detail** The sand and foliage at the bottom of the image have fallen too dark and are dragging the eye downwards from the rest of the scene. Restore some balance by brushing parts of the adjustment out with a large, soft black brush set to 40% Opacity and the layer mask still active. Repeat for any other areas as needed.

04 **Boost contrast with Curves** To boost contrast a little, add a Curves adjustment layer using the button at the base of the Layers palette. Plot a point in the shadows and one in the highlights. Pull the shadow point down a fraction and push the highlight one up fairly hard to really let those bright tones sing.

05 **Darken the sky** The sky is too bright at the top and is pulling the eye upwards. To better balance the tonal range of the scene, add a Curves adjustment layer and pull downwards with a single point. Press 'G' for the Gradient tool and drag from the top of the sky to the horizon for a dramatically darkened edge.

06 **Colour the beach** The sand looks a rather greenish colour and needs to be brought in line with the orange glow elsewhere in the image. Add a Color Balance adjustment layer and, with Midtones selected, set Cyan/Red to +40 and Yellow/Blue to -65. Invert the mask with Cmd/Ctrl+I and paint into the beach with a white brush.

07 **Alter yellows** Now we're ready to play with colour a little. Start by adding a Hue/Saturation adjustment layer. We know that our image is made up predominantly of yellows and blues so we can make alterations to colour by working these colour ranges. Select Yellows from the drop-down menu to start and shift Hue to -15 to drive the yellows toward an orange-pink.

08 **Alter the blues** We push Saturation to +8 to increase colour. Now select Blues and push Hue to -23 for a more turquoise colour. Pushing the Hue slider in Cyans to -15 gives an interesting tint to the lower sky. Change the layer blending mode to Color to prevent the lightness being affected.

"There are a number of clever ways to simulate the colour and texture of old imagery"

Start image

Create a vintage photograph

Create an antique-photograph effect with real vintage paper

There are many techniques kicking around the web that instruct you how to make an image look like a vintage photograph from great grandpa's personal collection. There are a number of clever ways to simulate the colour and texture of old imagery with various filter effects, but not one of them comes close to using a photograph of the real thing. If you have an image of old paper or parchment with nothing else on, you can add your picture to the paper and watch it quietly seep in with some clever blending mode tricks. Add a bit of Levels fade and the result is 100 per cent authentic.

Play with blend modes

Whenever you use blending modes, always try some other ones out just to see if you have a 'happy accident' and discover a whole new look. We used Overlay in the example below, which gives a fantastic vintage effect.

USE LAYER BLENDING MODES TO COMBINE TWO IMAGES

Old plus new equals old!

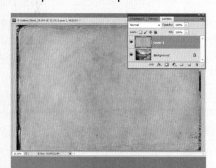

01 Copy texture across Open up both of the start images for this effect – the canoeing scene and the vintage paper texture. Hold down Shift and drag the Background layer of the texture image across to the canoe image to make a copy of it.

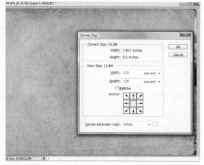

02 Extend the canvas Next, go to Image>Canvas Size and change the drop-down units to percent. Set the Height to 120 percent and the Width to 110 percent. Make sure the Canvas Extension colour is set to White then press Enter to apply the changes.

03 Free Transform With the texture layer active, use Cmd/Ctrl+T for a Free Transform and drag the handles so the texture layer fills the full canvas frame. Hit Enter twice, then change the blending mode to Multiply.

04 Tone the image Now duplicate the texture layer using Cmd/Ctrl+J with the layer selected. Change the blending mode from Normal to Color. This gives our image the same colour wash as the paper texture, effectively converting it to a black and white image with a sepia tone.

05 Add a Solid Color layer Next, double-click the Background layer to bring up the dialog and press Enter to rename the layer. This lets us place another layer underneath, ready for the edge trim that is coming next. Add a Solid Color adjustment layer, choose white and move it underneath the renamed Background layer.

06 Trim the image area Select the Background layer and choose the Polygonal Lasso tool. Click a selection around the image area, cutting off each of the corners a little as shown. Now go to Select>Modify>Smooth and Enter a value of 100px to smooth the edges.

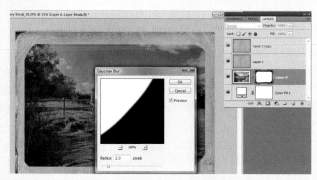

07 Feather the mask With the selection active, add a layer mask using the button at the base of the Layers palette and watch the corners disappear. They still look a little too sharp, so select the layer mask and go to Filter>Blur>Gaussian Blur. Use 1-2px.

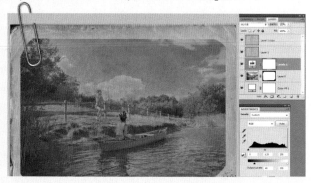

08 Fade the image Finally, add a Levels adjustment layer above the Background. Set the bottom black slider to 40 to fade the shadow tones, and the middle top slider to 1.25 to lighten the image as a whole for a different type of fade.

Convert to duotone

Quickly add a classy look to your images

You can get up to all sorts of creative tasks in Photoshop, but one of the most satisfying is replicating traditional film camera effects in minutes.

Duotone, or split-toning, is a traditional process whereby toning chemicals are used to add a colour sheen to black-and-white images. The chemicals can be set to target either shadows or highlights and result in a classic look. Photoshop has a dedicated Duotone command, making it a breeze to try the effect yourself.

Top tip: If you want to accentuate areas even more, use the Dodge or Burn tools to emphasise light and shadow.

QUICK FIX

Before

After

FROM FULL COLOUR TO DUO COLOUR
Three steps are all you need

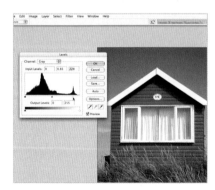

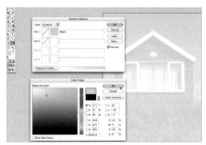

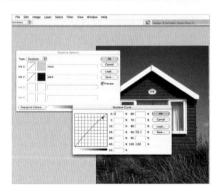

01 Go grey To begin your duotone odyssey, you need to prep your start image. Open it in Photoshop and then go to Image>Mode>Grayscale. If this ends up looking a little flat, take a trip to the Levels or Curves to bring back some punch.

02 Add colour Back to the Image menu but this time go to Mode>Duotone. This will open up a special dialog. Select Duotone from the Type: drop-down menu a nd then click the colour square for Ink 1 and pick a hue from the picker. Repeat for Ink 2. You'll be shown a colour library for Ink 2, but you can click the Color Picker button if you prefer that method.

03 Curve control Before you click OK, you will need to add a name to each of your ink colours. Each ink also has an adjustable curve. Click the square with the diagonal line in it to bring up a curve. Now alter the tone of each of your colours using this method.

Add a faded vignette to photos

Here's a quick and easy treatment to make portraits really stand out

Sometimes you can capture the perfect expression of somebody in a photo, only to discover that the rest of the scene is ugly or distracting.

By adding a faded vignette to your subject, you will be able to eliminate all the background activity from your shot, while giving your portrait a lovely soft glow. It's easy to apply, and the results will make your images look professional.

This technique is also great if you want to blend a couple of images together on a page. Simply add another layer filled with colour or texture beneath your portrait and see your image blend smoothly.

Top tip: Use a texture photo from a stock site as a great background for your image.

Before

After

CREATE A BEAUTIFUL FADE ON PHOTOS
A simple technique to dramatically improve your portraits

01 Make a selection Open your photo and double-click the Background layer to make it active. Now select the Elliptical Marquee tool from the toolbar and draw a shape around the area of the photo you want to keep. Anything outside the circle will not be visible.

02 Apply a mask Next, add a layer mask by clicking on the white circular icon at the foot of the Layers palette. There are two thumbnails on this layer – make sure that the layer mask thumbnail is active by clicking on it.

03 Create the fade In the menu bar go to Filter>Blur>Gaussian Blur. A dialog box will appear with a preview window. Ensure the Preview option is ticked and then alter the Radius setting to suit your image. Now you can add any background you wish to your image, by placing a new layer underneath and using the Fill tool to colour it.

Before make-up

Digital make-up

Learn how to glam up your beauty portraits with this digital make-up tutorial

If you're after a professional make-up look for your portraits but don't want the mess, why not have a go digitally? With a bit of patience and practice you can achieve some very realistic looks for applying make-up in Photoshop, and it only takes a matter of minutes to do.

The key here is subtlety, unless you're painting a clown's face! So we'll be using plenty of layers and soft brushes, and experimenting with different blending modes.

We'll start by creating a base colour or foundation – in this case a slightly darker colour of the original skin tone. We'll use the Color blending mode to maintain skin texture underneath. The Dust and Scratches filter will be used with a mask to selectively smooth out areas of the skin and help draw emphasis towards features like the eyes and lips. We will selectively lighten and add contrast to the eyes, using adjustment layers and curves. Curves will also be used to darken features and tones to simulate eyeliner and eye shadow.

We'll create a two-coloured eye shadow using soft brushes with the Overlay and Color blending modes, and add a subtle cherry lipstick using the same technique. We'll even add further eyelashes to the model using stroked paths, and then blend them with the existing eyelashes before rounding things off with some Contrast and Saturation adjustments using Gaussian Blur and the Soft Light mode.

TIME TO GLAM UP
Give the model a digital makeover

01 **Applying foundation** Let's start with foundation. Go to Layer>New Layer, select a soft brush (B) and choose a brown colour as the foreground from the swatches. At the top of the Layers palette select the Color blending mode and start painting over the skin. Reduce the layer's Opacity to 45%.

02 **Smoothing skin** Go to Layer> Duplicate Layer then Filter>Dust and Scratches. Choose 4 for the Radius and 11 for the Threshold. Click on the Add Layer Mask icon (circle and square icon) at the bottom of the Layers palette. With the mask selected, paint in black over the eyes, lips, eyebrows and hair to bring back the original layer.

03 **Draw eyelashes** Create a new layer, zoom into the right eye. Select the Path tool (P) and click to add a point at the base of the eyelashes. Click another point, hold down the mouse and drag. This creates a curve. Hold down the Cmd/Ctrl key and click and drag the handle to adjust.

04 **Stroke eyelashes** Cmd/Ctrl-click an empty space and repeat. Hit the Brush tool (B) and choose a Width of 2px with a hard edge. Pick a dark brown. Select the Pen tool (P) and Cmd/Ctrl-click and drag to select the paths. Hit Stroke Path in the Paths menu. Reduce the layer's Opacity to blend with existing lashes.

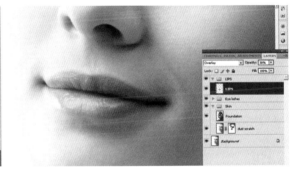

05 **Adding lipstick** Create a new layer. Select a soft brush and choose a dark cherry red for the lipstick colour. Set the layer blending mode to Overlay and paint over the lips. Reduce the layer's Opacity to 30%. Next, click on the Add Layer Mask icon at the bottom of the Layers palette and choose Curves.

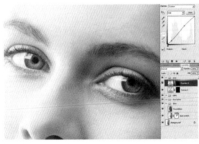

06 **Eye contrast** Now click on the middle of the curve and drag upwards to lighten. Click on the layer mask and press Cmd/Ctrl+I to invert the mask to black. Next, with a white brush, paint over the eyes to lighten them. Add another Curves adjustment layer, and this time draw a subtle 'S' shape for contrast. Repeat masking techniques.

07 **Adding eye shadow** Create a new layer and choose a soft brush with a bright yellow colour. Change the blending mode to Color and paint around the bottom and top of the eyelids. Reduce the layer's Opacity to blend. You may need to add the Gaussian Blur filter to soften. Repeat using the Darken blending mode and grey for the shadow. Try a layer with grey in Overlay mode.

08 **Eyeliner and darkening** Create a new Curves adjustment layer for the eyeliner. Pull down on the curve to darken and then invert the mask as before. Use a small brush to paint in eyeliner. Repeat the process for eye shadow and adjust the opacity to blend. Repeat for the eyebrows and repeat the lipstick step to add blusher to the cheeks.

Before

After

Tips & fixes

Make your own texture

As long as you have a camera, you have the ability to create your own textures. From peeling paint to straw baskets, texture is all around us. Simply set your camera to Macro mode (represented by a flower icon), set the flash to Off and then take your shot. Keep your textures in a folder on your computer – you never know when they might come in handy.

Add texture to photos

Transform your dull, grey landscape photographs using a gorgeous textured sky

We've all got plenty of landscape photos that would be rather beautiful if it weren't for the dull, washed-out overcast sky. It seems a shame not to celebrate these images just because of the weather, so here's a nifty little tutorial that makes the most of those dull, uninteresting skies.

In just eight steps we'll introduce you to the power of blending modes, as well as give you a simple lesson in using layer masks. Both these skills can be applied to a host of other projects, so try and store the techniques to memory.

We'll be incorporating some great texture into the sky to give your image depth and interest. This tutorial works best with landscape images that have a fairly flat, plain horizon, as it makes life a whole lot easier when combining the two images together. However, in this tutorial we've chosen a slightly more challenging

horizon to enable you to get accustomed to using layer masks. Texture is a fantastic resource to use in your Photoshop designs, as it adds depth, interest and a tactile quality. We recommend you get out there and start photographing your own texture images, so

"Start photographing your own texture images so you can build up an archive you can dip into"

you can build up an impressive archive you can dip into at any time. Before you begin you will need to find a suitable start image and a texture to work with.

TRANSFORM THE LANDSCAPE
Find out what blending modes can do

01 Gather your images Open your landscape photo. Images with an uncluttered horizon and overcast sky work best. Drag your textured paint file onto your landscape file. Double-click the new layer, name it 'Texture', go to Edit>Transform>Scale and make the texture fit the width of the canvas. Hit Enter.

02 Line them up With the Texture layer active, select the Move tool from the top of the toolbar and position the texture image so it sits directly on the horizon level of your landscape image.

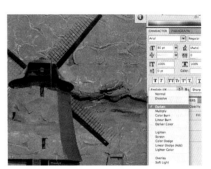

03 Combine your pics At the top of the Layers palette use the drop-down menu to alter the blending mode from Normal to Darken. This will select the darkest pixels, enabling your landscape image to show through the Texture layer.

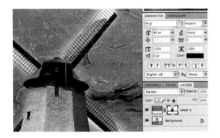

04 Smooth it out Keep the Texture layer active and add a layer mask. Choose a soft brush, set the foreground colour to black and Opacity to 100%. Use this brush to smooth over the hard line created by the Texture layer and rescue any lost detail, including the windmill's blades. Don't worry if they look messy, we'll tidy them up in Step 8.

05 Reclaim sky detail If your image doesn't have clouds, go to Step 7. If it does, let's have them show through the texture. Activate the background layer and select the sky with the Rectangular Marquee tool. Hit Cmd/Ctrl+J to turn this selection into a layer. Drag it to the top of the Layers palette, name it 'Clouds' and set the blending mode to Multiply.

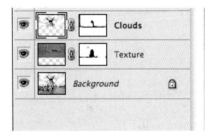

06 More masking The Multiply blending mode makes your image quite dark, so add another layer mask to the Clouds layer and once again use your black brush to blend the lower part of the sky. This will help you merge the landscape and texture together. Brush over the top of the windmill to lighten it up a bit.

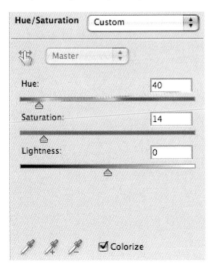

07 Make it succinct To give your image a more succinct feel, let's add an adjustment layer to the piece. Hit the black and white icon at the bottom of the Layers palette and pick Hue/Saturation. Ensure that Colorize is checked, then set Saturation to 14, Hue to around 40. Click OK and add a Color blending mode set to 80% Opacity.

08 Tidy up Your image is almost complete, but we need to tidy those messy white bits left by the layer mask. Go to your Texture layer and click on the layer mask thumbnail. Set your soft brush to 100% Opacity and set the foreground colour to white. Now paint over any white parts of the windmill blades and anywhere else that needs texture restored.

Dreamy photo effects

Combine the Blur filter and blending modes to produce a soft and dreamy photo effect

If you're looking for a quick way to give photographs a boost, then you can't get much quicker than this. By adding a touch of blur along with a carefully chosen blending mode, you can produce soft, dreamy images in a flash. Check out these three quick steps to see how it's done.

QUICK FIX

Top tip: Try and experiment with other blending modes to achieve more great effects.

Before

After

LOOKING DREAMY
A photo effect that can be created in minutes

01 Double up Open your image and go to Image>Mode>RGB. Now drag the background layer onto the Create New Layer tab at the bottom of the Layers palette. You can rename this layer by double-clicking on it.

02 Add some blur Head to Filter>Blur> Gaussian Blur, and a new window will appear. Enter 15px and watch how the image changes in the preview window. You can alter the amount as you wish – just ensure the basic facial outlines are visible. Now hit OK.

03 Finishing touch With the top layer still selected, set the blending mode to Overlay using the drop-down at the top of the Layers palette. Your photo will take on a whole new appearance. To reduce the redness, just click on the black and white circle at the bottom of the Layers palette, choose Hue/ Saturation and set Hue to +3, Saturation to -2 and Lightness to 0. Click OK.

Create a Lomo effect

Re-create a traditional photographic style for extra drama

Although we work within the digital realm, there is lots of inspiration to be found by looking at traditional photographic effects. Whether it's a processing style or a camera type, paying homage to retro looks can be a great way to get more from your images. Here we look at a quick and easy method for replicating the Lomo (or Lomography) style. Traditionally created with a Lomography camera, the technique is recognised for its strong, contrasting colours and vignette corners. You can still buy Lomo cameras relatively cheaply but it's cheaper still to create the effect in Photoshop! And here's how it's done.

Top tip: If you have CS2 or above, use the Vignette option within the Lens Correction filter (found in Distort).

Before

After

ADD DRAMA TO YOUR PHOTOS
Going loco for some Lomo

01 Vignette creation Open your photo and create a new layer by clicking on the button in the Layers palette. Select the Elliptical Marquee tool and draw around your focal point. Go to Select>Inverse, then Edit>Fill and choose Black from the Use: drop-down menu. Click OK and then deselect (Cmd/Ctrl+D).

02 Blur the boundaries The effect is too harsh at the moment, so head on up to Filter>Gaussian Blur, make sure the Preview box is checked and then use the Radius slider to alter the edges of the vignette. You want a soft effect. When happy, click OK and reduce the layer's Opacity to 70-75%.

03 Colour pop Click on your photo layer – it's time to make the colours sing! The most straightforward way is to use Curves and create an 'S' shape. If this is no good, call up the Brightness/Contrast tool and adjust the Contrast. Alternatively, go for some good old-fashioned Hue/Saturation to boost the tones.

Get creative

File Edit Image Layer Select Filter View Window Help

Feather: 0 px   Anti-alias   Style: Normal

Last Filter   ⌘F

Extract...   ⌥⌘X
Filter Gallery...
Liquify...   ⇧⌘X
Pattern Maker...   ⌥⇧⌘X
Vanishing Point...   ⌥⌘V

Artistic   ▶
Blur   ▶
Brush Strokes   ▶
Distort   ▶
Noise   ▶
Pixelate   ▶
Render   ▶
Sharpen   ▶
Sketch   ▶
Stylize   ▶
Texture   ▶
Video   ▶
Other   ▶

Digimarc   ▶

Average
Blur
Blur More
Box Blur...
Gaussian Blur...
Lens Blur...
Motion Blur...
Radial Blur...
Shape Blur...
Smart Blur...
Surface Blur...

Gaussian Blur
This filter gives a soft blur over the entire image, making it appear as if it was taken out of focus

Blur More
A very gentle blur is added to reduce overly sharp edges, although this is not very noticeable

Box Blur
Box Blur creates a blur that's shaped into a square of a chosen size

Surface Blur
Use the Surface Blur to add a soft focus effect to portraits to make a dream-like picture

Smart Blur
Smart Blur is ideal for reducing digital noise and smoothing out the edges

Shape Blur
Using the Custom Shapes tool in Photoshop, the Shape Blur filter blurs an image to a specific outline

Get creative with

Blur filters

Discover the Blur filters and find out how they can transform your photos

Blurring an image is probably not something you do very often, but there are a handful of reasons why you should think about Photoshop's Blur filters, and how they can be put to good use to enhance your photos.

You're likely to have seen many of the blur effects in your everyday life, but they're not obvious at first. This is because blurring techniques are usually there to help draw attention away from one subject and onto another. For example, if an image has an ugly background, this could be blurred to make it more appealing, and make the main subject the central focus. Blurring subjects is not only

Lens Blur
Lens Blur is perfect for depth of field, as it closely resembles the natural effect of a camera lens

Motion Blur
This filter adds movement to an image, and the angle can be altered to any direction

Radial Blur
Radial Blur is great for turning a static object into a spinning one, using either a Zoom or Spin effect

Original photo

Using Blur filters

It's rare for a Blur filter to look realistic without help from other tools. These include layer masks and feathering techniques. Follow the four steps below for a rundown on the best tools to make a blur look just right

01 Quick selections The Magic Wand tool is great for making a selection around a subject. Try to be as accurate as possible, but the beauty of Blur filters means that selections don't always need to be meticulous for them to work well.

02 Soften a selection Selections can benefit from having smooth and faded edges. Once a selection has been made, head to Select>Modify>Feather, and set to 10px. This number will change the amount of softening.

03 Layer masking To make a selection editable it's best to transform it into a layer mask. Duplicate the original image's layer, and with the selection still active click on the Add Layer Mask button in the Layers palette.

04 Time to blur Photoshop's collection of Blur filters can be found under the Filter menu. Each filter has been designed for a specific style of image, and here we've added a Motion Blur for movement.

an excellent way to hide ugly subjects, but also to soften the people in portrait images. You can use the Surface Blur filter on a person to take out harsh edges and graininess.

The group of Blur filters is found within the Filter menu (Filter>Blur), and they range from the popular Gaussian Blur to the dynamic Shape Blur. Most of the Blur filters use a dialog box that pops up to give you lots of control over the extent of the effect, along with a preview box, before you hit OK. Always ensure the preview is on so that you can see what each Blur filter does – the images above are a good guide too.

Blur filters can be used to add movement to static subjects or fake the effect of moving

car lights at night. The filters are extremely adaptable, as they can work with all sorts of tools, including the Pen, Brush and Selection tools. Selection tools are especially useful, letting you apply a Blur filter to a specific area. Combine this with a layer mask and you have lots of control over the shape of the blurry areas. A prime example of this is when it comes to creating depth of field, a technique in which you decide how much of the scene is in focus.

The Blur filters offer numerous creative opportunities, so let's look at some of the great things they can do over the next eight pages.

Use Blur filters to create depth of field

Depth of field happens naturally in all cameras, but if you don't own a camera with a flashy lens or manual controls it's much harder to achieve – and this is where Photoshop comes in. The idea of the effect is very simple – to blur different parts of the image in order to make one subject stand out over the rest. To better understand this effect, imagine a blurred image with every object indiscernible from the next. Now picture an invisible wall in focus, cutting across your image, and whatever this wall touches is made pin-sharp. It's a gradual effect and fades out at the closest and furthest points away from the eye.

The effect works better in images with close foregrounds and interesting backdrops. It also works well with close-up photos, and here we've used Photoshop's Lens Blur filter to transform this picture of a flower with a depth-of-field effect.

The Lens Blur filter works best for injecting depth of field into an image; select the area before applying the effect

01 Make a selection Drag the image's layer onto the Create New Layer button to duplicate it. With the Magnetic Lasso tool, make a selection around the middle of the flower. Once the selection is complete, Ctrl/right-click inside the area and choose Save Selection. Leave the Name field blank and hit OK. The selection will be saved in the Channels palette as 'Alpha 1'.

> "The idea of the effect is very simple – to blur different parts of the image in order to make one subject stand out over the rest"

02 Compose Hit Cmd/Ctrl+D to deselect the selection. Now's a good time to crop your image. Using the Crop tool, cut out the surrounding area to give the strongest composition. We removed the background in our flower image.

03 Add your blur To feather the selection, Cmd/Ctrl-click the thumbnail of the Alpha 1 layer in the Channels palette. Click the Quick Mask box in the toolbar ('Q'). Head to Filter>Blur>Gaussian Blur and set Radius to 50px – but this depends how blurry you want the depth of field to be. Hit OK, then hit 'Q' to exit Quick Mask mode.

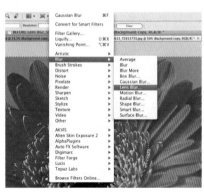

04 Blur some more With the selection active, go to Select> Inverse. To create the depth of field go to Filter>Blur>Lens Blur, and a separate menu should pop up. The Lens Blur filter is only available in Photoshop CS version and above. For earlier versions, the Gaussian Blur filter at a low value is the best alternative.

After
Soft focus in portraits can be made using the Surface Blur and Motion Blur filters in Photoshop combined with blend modes

Before

Average
Blur
Blur More
Box Blur...
Gaussian Blur...
Lens Blur...
Motion Blur...
Radial Blur...
Shape Blur...
Smart Blur...
Surface Blur...

05 Set the Radius In the Lens Blur menu tick the Preview button. Everything around the selection should turn blurry. In the Iris section of the menu, set Shape to Hexagon and change the Radius value until you're happy with the amount of blur. We used a Radius value of 45.

06 Masking Hit OK when you are pleased with the level of blurriness. Try and keep a subtle definition in the blurry areas to prevent the image becoming too abstract. The depth of field effect may need tidying up around the edges, so with the duplicate layer selected click on the Add Layer Mask button in the Layers palette.

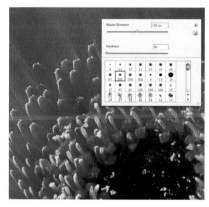

07 Finish up Select the layer mask's white thumbnail in the Layers palette. In the toolbar, set the foreground colour to black and background colour to white. With the Brush tool set to Soft Edge, paint away parts of the blurred transition to reveal detail underneath for a tidier depth of field effect.

Surface Blur filter

We recommend using a portrait image for this effect. Duplicate the image layer to make adjustments non-destructively and head to Filter>Blur>Surface Blur. This only works in CS versions and above; for earlier versions use Noise>Median instead. In the Surface Blur menu set the values 15 for Radius and 30 for Threshold. Your subject's skin should smooth out and look almost painted.

Overlay blending

To add more contrast and impact to the soft focus effect, go to the Layers palette where you should have the duplicated layer with the blur applied. Drag this layer onto the Add New Layer button to duplicate it again. On the new duplicated layer, go to the list of blend modes in the Layers palette and add the Overlay option. Your image will now look bolder and punchier in the shadows and highlights.

Enhance the soft focus

To make the effect a little easier on the eyes, reduce the contrast of the Overlay blend mode by lowering the Opacity of the layer to 80%. For the final touch we need to soften the image more. Go to Filter>Blur>Motion Blur and give it a Distance of 20 pixels and change its Angle to 0 degrees. Although this blur is mostly to add movement to an image, it works wonders for softening images of people.

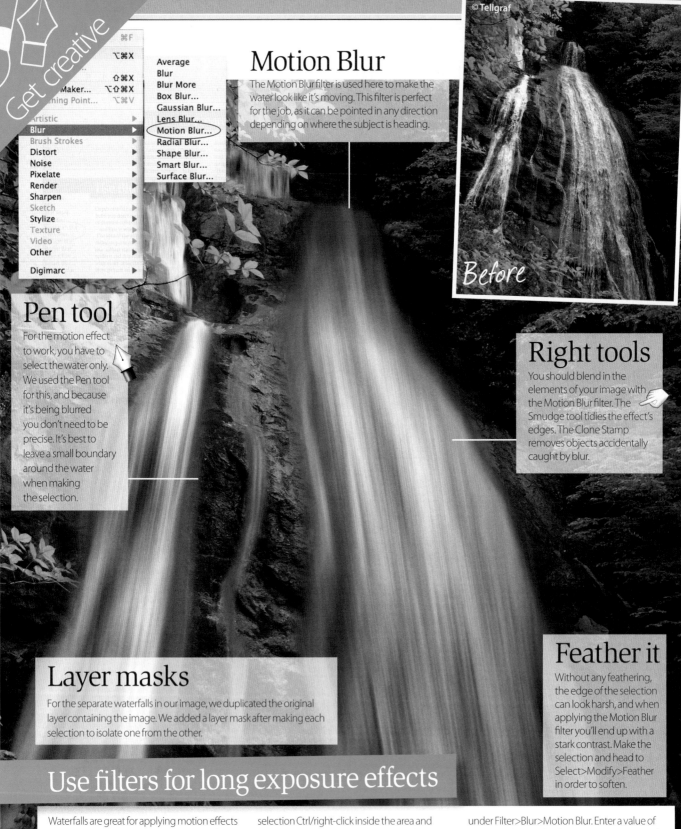

©Tellgraf

Before

Menu (partial)

⌘F
⌥⌘X
⇧⌘X
…Maker... ⌥⇧⌘X
…hing Point... ⌥⌘V

Artistic ▶
Blur ▶
Brush Strokes ▶
Distort ▶
Noise ▶
Pixelate ▶
Render ▶
Sharpen ▶
Sketch ▶
Stylize ▶
Texture ▶
Video ▶
Other ▶

Digimarc ▶

Average
Blur
Blur More
Box Blur...
Gaussian Blur...
Lens Blur...
Motion Blur...
Radial Blur...
Shape Blur...
Smart Blur...
Surface Blur...

Motion Blur

The Motion Blur filter is used here to make the water look like it's moving. This filter is perfect for the job, as it can be pointed in any direction depending on where the subject is heading.

Pen tool

For the motion effect to work, you have to select the water only. We used the Pen tool for this, and because it's being blurred you don't need to be precise. It's best to leave a small boundary around the water when making the selection.

Right tools

You should blend in the elements of your image with the Motion Blur filter. The Smudge tool tidies the effect's edges. The Clone Stamp removes objects accidentally caught by blur.

Layer masks

For the separate waterfalls in our image, we duplicated the original layer containing the image. We added a layer mask after making each selection to isolate one from the other.

Feather it

Without any feathering, the edge of the selection can look harsh, and when applying the Motion Blur filter you'll end up with a stark contrast. Make the selection and head to Select>Modify>Feather in order to soften.

Use filters for long exposure effects

Waterfalls are great for applying motion effects to accentuate movement. This motion effect is normally made using a long exposure in a camera. We used the Pen tool to make the selections around each watery part, one after the other. When drawing each selection, make it slightly bigger than the water itself. The Pen tool creates a path, and to convert this to a selection Ctrl/right-click inside the area and choose Make Selection. We duplicated the original layer for each new selection and also added a layer mask for each one. This is because all the waterfalls in our image move in slightly different directions, so we could edit them separately. Feather each selection by 25px (Select>Modify>Feather), then find the filter under Filter>Blur>Motion Blur. Enter a value of 200px and an Angle relating to the direction of the water. To smarten up the effect and ensure the blur is pointing in the right direction, use the Smudge tool at a low opacity to blend and move the edges around. If there are any plants in front of the waterfall, use the Clone Stamp tool to remove blurry leaves.

Get creative

After

Average
Blur
Blur More
Box Blur...
Gaussian Blur...
Lens Blur...
Motion Blur...
Radial Blur...
Shape Blur...
Smart Blur...
Surface Blur...

Before

Create a 'zoom tunnel'

Zoom tunnel effects are great for exaggerating movement where the subject is almost flying out of the camera. The filter to use is hidden in the Filter menu, under Radial Blur; select Zoom from the dialog box

01 Apply Zoom blur
Duplicate the image's layer and go to Filter>Blur>Radial Blur. Under Blur Method select the Zoom option to give the effect of a blurred tunnel. Position the blur in the correct place, and set Amount to 100. Now hit OK.

02 Layer masking
So that we can see the in-focus layer of our snowboarder and to make any adjustments undo-able, select Add Layer Mask in the Layers palette on the blurred image. Now select the Brush tool.

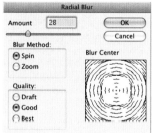

Creating motion blur

Before

To add movement to an image, isolate a subject and apply the Radial Blur filter. Adding movement to static objects can make photos more interesting. The first step is to duplicate the layer your image is on. The Radial Blur filter we're about to use works best on subjects with a flat perspective.

Use the Elliptical Marquee tool to drag a circle over the wheel. Go to Filter>Blur>Radial Blur. For blurring the wheel, choose Spin. Set the Amount to 28px, ensure the blur is placed in the middle of the preview window. Hit OK, then Cmd/Ctrl+D.

03 Prepare the Brush tool
Before we use the Brush tool to bring the in-focus image through, Ctrl/right-click on your image and set the Brush to 0% Hardness. Choose a large Brush Size, around 400px.

After

On the blurred layer, use the Eraser tool to remove parts outside the wheel that shouldn't be blurred. If there are spots that didn't blur, carefully use the Blur tool on the original layer to blend these in with the existing parts. Use the Smudge tool, set to Strength 50%, to add extra flare to the centre of the blur to emphasise speed.

04 Zoom effect finale
With the white layer mask thumbnail selected, begin to paint over the parts of your image that you want to make focused. This will now be the main subject, in a blurry tunnel of action!

	⌘F
Average	
Blur	
Blur More	
Box Blur...	
Gaussian Blur...	
Lens Blur...	
Motion Blur...	
Radial Blur...	
Shape Blur...	
Smart Blur...	
Surface Blur...	

⌥⌘X
⇧⌘X
... Maker... ⌥⇧⌘X
...shing Point... ⌥⌘V

Artistic ▶
Blur ▶
Brush Strokes ▶
Distort ▶
Noise ▶
Pixelate ▶
Render ▶
Sharpen ▶
Sketch ▶
Stylize ▶
Texture ▶
Video ▶
Other ▶

Digimarc ▶

Use Blur filters to create lights at night

We've all seen them, a night shot of a street in a city flooded with heavy traffic, and the lights of the cars spread from one side of the image to the other. The blurriness of the lights is created using a long exposure at night-time, and that same effect can be recreated in Photoshop even if there are no cars in the image.

The Box Blur filter works best for this particular technique, and it's very similar to the Gaussian Blur filter. The difference is subtle, but the Box Blur filter moulds the blur into a square, which imitates the lights of cars.

In this project we will imitate the flow of traffic with Box Blur, and also use Gaussian Blur to bring the street lights to life and give them a warm orange glow. Open up your start image (any traffic shot will work) and follow the steps below to find out how to create blurry traffic.

Before

© Matteo Discardi www.1802.it

After
The Pen tool and Box Blur filter together make perfect streams of light for imaginary traffic

01 **Car lights**
Create a new blank layer and select the Brush tool. Give it a red colour, make Size 10px and Hardness 100%. Now select the Pen tool and draw a single, curved line starting in the distance and finishing in the foreground. Ctrl/right-click on the line and select Stroke Path. Pick the Brush from the list.

02 **Box Blur filter** Go to Filter>Blur>Box Blur to soften the red line. Give the Box Blur a Radius of 6px and hit OK. To brighten the line's colour, drag its layer onto the Create New Layer button, and then hit Cmd/Ctrl+E to merge the two line layers.

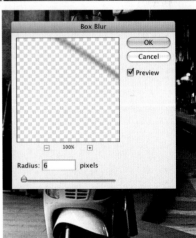

Use blur for abstract light effects

Blur filters can be used for many styles of art, and this can even include creating colourful, abstract lighting just like this.

To start with, create a new document with a black canvas. It's important to remember to create a new layer for every new line and shape you make. With the Elliptical Marquee tool, draw a circle then Ctrl/right-click in its centre and select Stroke. Select a vibrant yellow and a Width of around 20px, and hit OK. Hit Cmd/Ctrl+D to deselect, go to Filter>Blur>Radial Blur, and set this to an Amount of about 60 and to Spin. This creates a dynamic shape – but try this formula for different shapes.

The Pen tool can be especially useful. Draw a swirl shape with the Pen tool then Ctrl/right-click on the lines and select Stroke Path. Go to Filter>Blur>Gaussian Blur and add a subtle blur. Lay the lines on top of the shapes just made and set the blend mode to Overlay from within the Layers palette. If the lines and shapes appear faint, simply duplicate them and then hit Cmd/Ctrl+E to merge together.

Average
Blur
Blur More
Box Blur...
Gaussian Blur...
Lens Blur...
Motion Blur...
Radial Blur...
Shape Blur...
Smart Blur...
Surface Blur...

During

After
You can have a lot of fun with the Pen, Brush and Free Transform tools combined with the Gaussian Blur filter

> "In this project we will imitate the flow of traffic with Box Blur, and also use Gaussian Blur to bring the street lights to life"

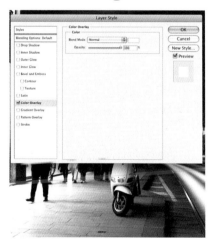

03 **Distort** To give the line more perspective, go to Edit>Transform> Distort. Bend the line until it resembles a beam of light from a car headlight. Duplicate this layer, move it and continue free transforming to create a pair of car lights.

04 **White beams** Duplicate again and move to the other side of the road. Double-click the layer to open the Layer Styles menu. Add a Color Overlay set to white. The Smudge tool works amazingly well on blurred lines, and you can gently bend and extend parts of the lights to fit the image.

05 **Finishing touches** To amplify the effect of the lights in the city at night, we added colour to the street lamps along the road. With the Brush tool set to orange, add a blotch of paint about twice as big as the bulb. Go to Filter>Blur>Gaussian Blur and give it a value of about 15px depending on the size of the light. In the Layers palette, set the layer's blend mode to Screen to make the middle of the light white, leaving just the blurry glow. Repeat this process, creating a new layer for each streetlight.

Tips & fixes

Different effects

Creativity doesn't stop with just one blend mode. Instead of using Overlay, try other modes such as Multiply. This particular one makes your sunset appear darker. You can also go for the retro look by using Pin Light mode to blend the red colour in the gradient map with a brown overtone, similar to that of a sepia effect. Experiment with them all to find the one that looks the best.

Before

After

Create a sunset using Gradient Maps

Intensify colour in your sunset photos with this non-destructive method

The Gradient Maps option makes it possible to change colours in an image while retaining the individual highlights and shadows.

In this tutorial we've used a gradient map to enhance our image of a sunset that's not quite captured the vibrancy of the light hitting the clouds and water's surface. They are simple to apply, and work effectively when combined with Photoshop's blending modes.

Gradient Maps is under the Adjustment Layers option in the Layers palette. The maps can be used with options such as Curves to intensify highlights in an image. The trick with the adjustment layers lies with their individual masks, which appear every time you create a new one.

The gradient map, as its name suggests, creates a gradient with multiple colours that covers your image to account for every subject and light source. For this sunset effect, we've created a gradient with the colours red, orange and yellow, and then we let the adjustment layer do the hard work for us. It's also a great way to change a normal scene into a more fantasy-based image, by applying odd colours that you wouldn't normally expect to see.

Although there are many ways to change the tone of your image in Photoshop, the Gradient Maps option is one of the easiest and is non-destructive. Grab any landscape photo from your collection in order to begin the transformation.

ADD WARMTH TO YOUR SUNSET IMAGES
Combine Gradient Maps and blending modes for a polished effect

01 **Find the gradient map** Open the image that you want to work on. There's no need to make a copy of the layer, as a gradient map appears on its own one. Click the Create New Adjustment Layer button in the Layers palette, and select Gradient Map.

02 **Gradient Editor** The image turns to black and white, but not for long! The gradient map appears as a new layer, and has its own mask. Double-click on the left thumbnail on its layer to open up the Gradient Editor dialog box.

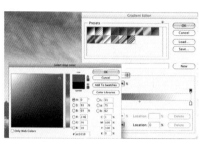

03 **A splash of red** In the Gradient Editor dialog box there are two squares on the bottom side of the gradient's colour bar. Double-click on the bottom left square (black by default). In the Select Stop Color box, choose a warm red and then hit OK to apply.

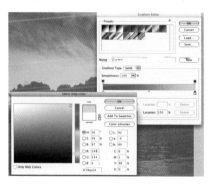

04 **A tint of yellow** Your image should tint red. To balance this, double-click on the far right square on the bottom side of the colour bar. Select a bright yellow and hit OK. The colour bar now has orange as the midtone, with red and yellow either side.

05 **Blend** Hit OK in the Gradient Editor menu to apply the mapping. The image will be a mix of orange, yellow and red. In the Layers palette, with the gradient map layer selected, change the blending to Overlay. This dramatically boosts the sunset's contrast.

06 **Tweak settings** To reduce the harshness of the gradient map created by the Overlay blend mode, use the Opacity slider in the Layers palette. Reduce its value to 60% to make the sunset subtle and more realistic. If the red is too dominant, go back to the Gradient Editor and pick a darker shade.

07 **Add some shimmer** To intensify the shimmer of the water, click on Curves in the New Adjustment Layer list in the Layers palette. Now pull the top of the line upwards in the Curves dialog box to give the image more brightness.

08 **Paint in light** Select the white thumbnail on the Curves adjustment layer, and go to Image>Adjustments>Invert. Use the Brush tool, set to black and a soft edge, to paint over the water to add shimmers of light coming from the horizon, completing your project.

Composing with Smart Objects

Intelligent editing with non-destructive results – Photoshop's Smart Objects explored and explained

Smart Objects first came with Photoshop CS2, and they made the editing process of a composition much easier. Smart Objects are controlled from inside the Layers palette, and are used to edit certain objects separately from the rest of the composition.

Sounds complicated, but Photoshop has made the process of editing Smart Objects simple. By double-clicking on a Smart Object's layer thumbnail, the object opens in a separate document for you to edit. This also applies to RAW files imported from a digital SLR. Using Smart Objects, RAW images can be edited separately at any point in your workflow.

There are other advantages to using Smart Objects for editing photos and objects, vector- or raster-based files. When a layer in your composition is converted to a Smart Object, it can be made smaller and then enlarged back to its original size without any loss of image definition – a major bonus if you're experimenting with the arrangement of your layers.

One of the main jobs of Photoshop's Smart Objects is to preserve the original quality of a layer, so that you can work in a non-destructive fashion. They can play a major role by connecting multiple layers together, and when one is edited, the other Smart Object layers are automatically updated with the changes.

Clipping masks/Smart Objects

When converting a layer to a Smart Object you're restricted to the adjustments in Image>Adjustments. With clipping masks you can use adjustment layers.

01 Unavailable options
When you've created a Smart Object, most of the adjustments in Image>Adjustments aren't available. Instead, head to the Layers palette with the Smart Object in and hit Create New Adjustment Layer.

02 Apply mask
Select an adjustment layer; we chose Levels to darken our ball object to bring it closer to the ambient lighting. Before making adjustments, Ctrl/right-click the adjustment layer and select Create Clipping Mask.

03 Set adjustments
The clipping mask makes sure that only the layer below is affected by any adjustments, and not the whole image. Making the necessary adjustments to an object can be changed at any time.

Smart editing
Repetitive editing made easy

If you're creating a composition consisting of multiple objects and need to apply the same edits to each one, you can convert one of these objects to a Smart Object (Layer>Smart Objects>Convert to Smart Object). Then simply duplicate the Smart Object's layer by dragging it onto the Create New Layer button as many times as you need. To edit one of the objects,

double-click the layer's thumbnail and your image object will open as a new document. Perform the necessary edits, go to File>Save, go back to your original composition and notice how all other objects have been updated automatically without the need to edit each one separately. You can also select all the original layers and create one Smart Object layer.

Scaling definition
Remembers original resolution

Smart Objects have many advantages for artists transforming and resizing images. Converting an image to a Smart Object (Ctrl/right-click on its layer and select Convert To Smart Object) allows you to resize

your image without losing image quality. For example, making a non-Smart Object very small using Photoshop's Free Transform, and then resizing the image back to its original size, the image becomes distorted and pixelated. But if you resize an image to small dimensions and back to its original with it set as a Smart Object, no distortion will occur.

Get control with brushes You can use any brush to apply a Quick Mask. We recommend you use a soft brush for details such as hair and fur – this will give you a softer, more subtle selection.

Finding Smart Object commands All the commands for Smart Objects are found under Layer>Smart Objects. Here you can convert, replace and export an image in the Smart Object, and also rasterize one to revert to a normal layer.

Clipping masks By adding a clipping mask onto an adjustment layer in the Layers palette, you can apply its changes only to the layer beneath. This method is particularly useful when you work with Smart Objects.

Smarter editing With our main images converted to Smart Objects, we have used Transform commands to shape them to the billboards without the risk of losing detail. By double-clicking on a Smart Object's layer thumbnail, each image can be edited separately in its original form.

Smart Objects Convert a layer to a Smart Object by Ctrl/right-clicking and selecting Convert to Smart Object. A converted layer indicates that it's a Smart Object by showing a small symbol on its thumbnail.

Tips & fixes

Smart Objects and layer masks
If you're creating a composite image and need to apply a selection with a layer mask, make sure you convert your image to a Smart Object before applying the layer mask.

Replace contents
Versatile editing

Among the many advantages to editing compositions using Smart Object layers is the ability to replace an object with a new one at any stage. With a Smart Object selected, head to Layer>Smart Objects>Replace and then pick an image that you want to put in its place. Once imported into your composition, because it's now a Smart Object it can shrink or enlarge back to the original without the fear of losing image definition. Such dramatic resizing with normal layers can destroy pixel definition and is only undo-able by stepping back in the History states.

Raw file editing
Get smart with Raw

If you take pictures using the RAW file format with a digital SLR, you can edit these using Adobe Camera Raw software, which pops up as you open Photoshop. You can convert RAW images into a Smart Object with Adobe Camera Raw by ticking the Open In Photoshop As Smart Objects option in the Workflow dialog box (via the underlined text at the base of the interface). This allows you to go back into Camera Raw by double-clicking the Smart Object's layer thumbnail in Photoshop.

Circular selections

Go beyond the normal selections and learn to create a perfect circle

The default selection that most people go for is a square or rectangle, but why not try something a bit different and pick a circle? This is a great way of drawing focus to your subject. The only problem here is that it is very difficult to make a perfect circle using the Elliptical Marquee tool and it can be even more difficult to make the selection over the area you need. But there is a quick fix for that, as we show you here.

QUICK FIX

Before

After

MAKE YOUR CIRCLE
Create a perfect ellipses every time

01 **A perfect circle** Select the Elliptical Marquee tool from the toolbar. Usually when you use this tool, it can be a bit hit and miss to make a perfect circle. To ensure that your circle is perfectly honed, hold down Shift as you drag out to keep the dimensions on track.

02 **Precise position control** If you want the selection to originate from a set point, hold down the Opt/Alt key and then click where you want the circle to originate from. Remember to hold down Shift if you want that perfect circle!

03 **Centre circle** If you need to find the centre of a document, go to Select>All and Edit>Free Transform. You'll see a crosshair at the centre of the document. Drag some guides to mark the point, press Esc to get out of Free Transform, and then Select>Deselect. Click on the middle mark, and use Opt/Alt key to originate from that point.

Set off some digital fireworks

Light up the skies of your photos using downloaded resources

Fireworks are always fantastic to watch, but they are slippery customers when it comes to taking quality photos. If you haven't got a tripod you can forget about it, but even if you have you aren't guaranteed a perfect shot. You need to get the timings just right, if there is pollution in the air you will just capture lots of smoke and if there are crowds you have that to contend with.

A far easier way is to create the fireworks in Photoshop and apply them to your photo. And the easiest way of all is to use fireworks that somebody else has made! We are using files from the Photoshop Daily site to add pizzazz to our sky

Top tip: Don't forget the reflections. Paste the firework onto the reflective surface and use a blending mode to make it look real.

CREATE A CELEBRATORY SCENE
All of the pyrotechnics, none of the fuss

01 **Select your area** We are going to be copying and pasting the fireworks into a photo, using selections to control where the fireworks appear. The first task is to make that selection. The sky of our photo is pretty uniform in colour, so we just need to select the Magic Wand tool and click in the sky.

02 **Add some fire** Go to www. photoshopdaily.co.uk/news/ firework-files and download the free firework files. These are PNG files, with all of the transparency intact. Open one up, Select All and then copy. Click on your firework photo (making sure the selection is still intact) and go to Edit>Paste Into to incorporate it.

03 **No overlap** The firework will appear on a new layer, only in the area that was selected. Go to Select>Deselect and use the Move tool to place it where you like and the Edit>Free Transform command to alter the size and angle of the firework. To add more, Cmd/Ctrl-click on the layer mask thumbnail in the Layers palette to reselect. Open another firework file then Copy and Paste Into as before.

Tips & fixes

Use negative space

While creating shapes for the vector mask frame, the predominant effort is taken by shaping the visible area, or positive space. By changing the path mode to Subtract From Path Area, you can use the shapes to form negative space that cuts into the image instead. This can be used to create a more interesting effect and help direct the viewer's eye. In our example here, the grass shapes at the bottom of the frame use negative space.

Stylish photo frames

Learn how to use masks and create custom border effects to spice up your photographs

For decades, photographers have known that one of the easiest ways to add spice and interest to a photo is to frame it. The very act of dressing the photo immediately elevates the visual appeal and often adds a much-needed finishing touch. And finding the right frame to enhance the mood and message is all part of the fun!.

In today's digital age, many people forget the importance of framing a photograph as it never makes it to print. If images are intended to be displayed digitally, usually they are frameless forever. But this doesn't need to be the case, and could in fact be to the image's detriment, as the very fact that you're working digitally introduces many more options for framing. The combination of

effects is limited only by your imagination. In this short tutorial we will show you how to use Photoshop to create two very different frame effects using two very different techniques.

The first will show how to create an intricate vector frame in a floral style that can be scaled up to fit any image size with no loss of detail (as is the beauty of vectors). The second technique will show how to create a custom border based on scans of paint splashes and brushstrokes for a more organic, dynamic look.

It is worth noting that both techniques require the image to be on its own, non-Background layer. If your image is on the Background, simply double-click the layer name to change it to a regular layer and make it editable before you begin the steps.

CREATE YOUR FAVOURITE FRAME STYLE
Use vector shapes or custom brushes for stunning borders

01 **Choose your path** Grab the Custom Shape tool (it's hiding behind the Rectangle shape tool). In the Options bar, press the icon for Paths instead of Shapes, then select a custom shape from the drop-down menu. Here, we used the Leaf 1 shape. Draw the shape over the part of the image you want to frame.

02 **Create the mask** Go to Layer>Vector Mask>Current Path to use the path to define the shape of the layer. Select the path using the Path Selection tool (the black arrow) and transform it as needed using the Edit>Transform Path commands. Use the Direct Selection tool (white arrow) to move or delete individual points.

03 **Additional shapes** Use the Custom Shape tool again, with the mode set to Add to Path Area to add more shapes to the frame. The shapes will all work together to form the frame, yet still be individual paths that can be selected, edited and copied.

04 **Fill out the frame** Continue adding and manipulating shapes until your frame is full. This technique makes it easy to create your shaped frame in as complex or simple a way as you want. Consider adding a Drop Shadow layer style for a bit more depth and an even more interesting effect.

05 **Create custom brushes** We have used a traditional paintbrush to create some 'splats' and scanned them in. We'll use these images to create our custom brushes. In each file, go to Edit>Define Brush Preset then close the files. You now have two, very high-resolution custom paint splatter brushes free for your own use.

06 **The humble layer mask** Open your photo, making sure it is not the Background layer. Add a new layer filled with black below the photo (or make the existing Background black). Click on the photo layer and create a rectangular selection. Press the Add Layer Mask button. This places a mask thumbnail next to the layer thumbnail.

07 **Use the custom brushes** Grab the Brush tool, set the paint colour to white, and use the PaintStroke preset defined previously as your tip. Be sure your Foreground is set to white. Open the Brushes palette (press F5) and adjust the size and angle to fit your image. Click on the canvas to deliver a paint stroke. Adjust the angle and stamp again until the entire frame is painted over.

08 **Add some flair** If you can still see the rectangular outline through the brushstrokes, reduce the brush size and carefully stamp out those areas. Then switch to the Splatter01 brush preset and repeat the process for some extra flair to your custom painted frame.

Use photos in type

Add 'pow' to your titles with this nifty trick

Clipping masks are a great way of placing objects inside other objects and can be used for all sorts of wild and wonderful things. Our example here may not be particularly wild, but it is a wonderful way of creating eye-catching titles.

The theory is simple; you begin with some type on a new document. You open up a photo, copy and paste a version of this into the type document and then use a clipping mask to make the photo magically appear inside the type. The most obvious use for this technique is in titles (it works especially well for fun digital scrapbooks and photobooks) or you could create an entire image made from text and photos.

Top tip: Don't be confined to type – use this technique to apply a photo to whatever shape or object you like.

Before

QUICK FIX

RELAX

KICK BACK WITH A CREATIVE TEXT EFFECT
Three simple steps to combine word and image

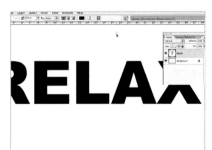

01 Make your type Create a new document and select the Type tool from the toolbar. Go up to the Font area and click to see the available fonts. Pick one that is a bit chunky (you want to see the photo, after all!). Click on your document and type your word.

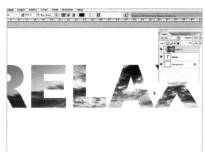

02 Photo time Open the photo you want to use, Select All and then copy. Click back on your type document and paste. It will appear above your type. Go to Layers>Create Clipping Mask and it will automatically cling to your text. You can reposition using the Move tool.

03 Outline To add more emphasis, double-click on the type layer to open the Layer Styles palette. Click the Stroke option at the bottom and then pick a colour and size. You can also return to the Background layer and use the Edit>Fill option to change the colour if you wish. We decided black would be more dramatic.

Quick cross processing

Emulate the popular film effect in the digital darkroom

QUICK FIX

Cross processing is an effect that was popular with traditional film, and it involved processing negatives in the wrong chemicals to get a particular effect. Usually, cross-processed images take on a desaturated and green-tinted effect. To get it right in the darkroom, it took trial and error, and a little bit of luck. Photoshop, however, can recreate the effect in just a couple of minutes, and should something go wrong it is easy to tweak the effect to suit without having to start all over again. The effect is created by using the Curves adjustment layer. We show you how it is done.

Top tip: Hit the Save button in the Curves dialog to save the curve to use again and again.

Before

After

SIMPLE CURVES
Use this essential tool to get the right look

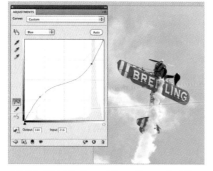

01 **Red and green need to be seen** Go to the bottom of the Layers palette and choose the New Adjustment layer button. Pick Curves. In the Curves dialog box, select the Red channel and create a soft 'S' with the curve line, as shown here. Do exactly the same thing with the Green channel selected.

02 **Upside down blues** Now select the Blue channel. This is the one that will help us to finalise our effect. Create an inverted 'S' curve this time, as shown in the screenshot. As we are using an adjustment layer, you can go back into the Curves layer and make as many tweaks to the channels as you like.

03 **Remove some colour** Now we need to add another adjustment layer, this time picking the Hue/Saturation option. We want to desaturate the image slightly to give the photo that retro look. We dragged the Saturation slider down to -12, but play with the values until you are happy.

Add sparkle to your brushes

Learn how to customise your brushes to really make them sparkle and shine

We all love a bit of sparkle in our lives, so why not use Photoshop to create your very own bespoke glitter brush?

In this tutorial you'll discover how to take an ordinary photo and add a gorgeous magical touch to it. You will learn the process of making a glitter type brush by manipulating the Photoshop default Circle brush. You'll also learn about lighting techniques in order to give your glitter brush some essential sparkle! This technique can be applied to any image or photograph that you want, so be sure to keep your newly created brush handy to apply it whenever you feel the need for a bit of magic.

You will call upon the brush settings such as Jitter, Size and Scatter to create the basic brush shape. Then it's a case of careful placement, colouring and blending to give it that touch of magic.

In this tutorial we have applied our glitter brush to a regular photo, which looks quite realistic, but you can ramp up the glitz and glam even more and use it in fantasy designs, text effects and even interesting backgrounds. This is a versatile brush that you'll be able to call upon again and again, and the best thing is that it's really easy to create using your existing brushes.

You can use any photograph that you like to recreate this effect, but why not start with a portrait like us?

CREATE SPARKLE EFFECTS!
Learn to create glowing sparkle effects and how to incorporate them into a photo

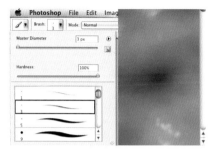

01 Choose a base brush The first step is for us to select the basic brush that we'll be using to create our sparkles. Select the Brush tool, and in the Options bar go up to the top left corner and open your Brush menu. Choose a Size 3 Hard Circular brush.

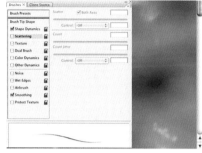

02 Brush settings Now we need to choose our brush settings. Check the box that says Scatter and enter these settings: Scatter 895%, Count 1, Jitter 100%. Leave the other settings as default.

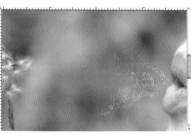

03 Get brushing Make sure your brush colour is a light white or yellow. Now zoom in close to the flower and click around to apply the brush. Try to brush in a direction to simulate the direction the model is blowing out from her mouth. Take your time to perfect this and get the shape right.

04 Size increase The next step is to simply increase the size of your brush to around 14. Now repeat the previous step and brush bigger sparkles over the smaller ones. The smaller ones help to add extra detail, whereas the larger ones help provide the coverage on your image.

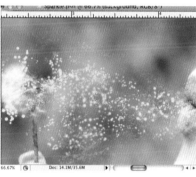

05 More dots Repeat Steps 3 and 4 until you're happy with the composition. Increase and decrease the brush size using the '[' and ']' keys and get some direction and flow going. The goal here is to simulate sparkles that are floating away.

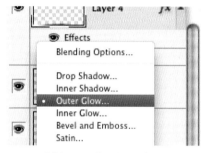

06 Add some glow Now it's time to make our dots glow and turn them into sparkles. Select your layer with all your dots on and then go to the Effects option at the bottom of the Layers palette. Check Outer Glow, set Opacity to 20% and set the blend mode to Screen. You can leave all the other settings as they are.

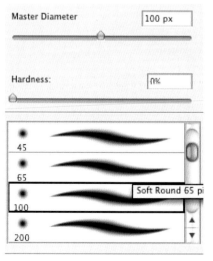

07 Gone with the wind Now choose a default 100 Size Soft Round brush. With 30% Opacity and white as your colour, draw soft lines from the flower outwards, showing wind from her blowing the sparkles outwards. Vary the opacity to suit your image.

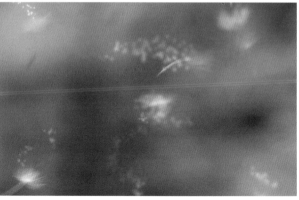

08 Add depth and movement Now let's create some depth and movement in our image. Following Steps 3 and 4, brush some sparkles in the distance. Now take the Blur tool and blur these sparkles to add depth and a sense of motion to the image.

Selection methods

There's more than one way to make a selection around a subject in Photoshop. Here we've used both the Magnetic Lasso and Quick Selection tools to separate the subject from the sky. But if this method doesn't suit your image, try using the Pen tool for the trickier areas of the subject. This tool takes more time than the ones used here, but you can bend and control each point with the Pen tool.

Start image

Create a silhouette in Photoshop

Learn how to turn an ordinary image into a funky silhouette using simple selections

Silhouettes are a great way of turning plain images, with not much happening in them, into bold and interesting compositions.

Caught in front of a sunset, on a stage with glowing lights behind the subject's head, or dancing in the moonlight – these are just a few situations where silhouettes occur. It's a captivating effect, and is popularly used for graphical artwork for contrasting with other colours.

In photography it's known as the 'backlit effect' and some cameras have the capability to automatically compensate for the lack of foreground light. However, Photoshop enables you to take full control of the lighting situation and every element within your image. With the help of a few fast Selection tools, multiple layers and colour adjustments, you can turn any area of your image into a dramatic silhouette.

If you go for the jet-black silhouette, it can lend itself to more abstract and graphical artwork. The blue sky background of our image for this tutorial actually better suits the black silhouette with a pinkish tone.

And if you've ever looked at a silhouette and wondered how to recreate the fantastic effect – well, now's your chance. In this tutorial we take you through the selection process and show you how to fill that area with black. Or you can go for an interesting spin on things and change the silhouette's colour completely!

A HIGH-FLYING SILHOUETTE
Use various Selection tools to create your silhouette

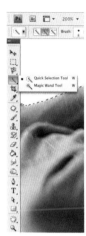

01 **Make a selection** Open the image that you want to work on. The first stage is to make a selection around the entire body of the subject. Select the Magnetic Lasso tool and in the Options bar make these adjustments: Width 5px, Contrast 10%, Frequency 50. Set Feather to 0px.

02 **Up close and personal** Zoom in to your image to 200% and click once with the Magnetic Lasso tool anywhere on the edge of the subject. Hover along the edge to carry on the selection. Hold down the Spacebar to move the image as you go. Join the ends to complete the selection.

03 **Complete selection** To select the holes in the subject where the sky is showing, choose the Quick Selection tool (CS3 users or higher) and give it a Brush Size of 30px. Hold down Opt/Alt, clicking on the sky areas to complete the selection. Alternatively, use the Magic Wand tool and click on the 'Add to selection' icon in the options bar. Simply select each hole.

04 **A clean silhouette** You should now have the entire subject selected. Head to Select>Modify>Expand, and in the dialog box enter a value of 2px, then hit OK. You should notice that the selection moves away from your subject by a tiny amount, making for a clean silhouette.

05 **Separate it from the sky** To completely separate the subject from the sky, go to Layer>New>Layer Via Copy. This takes the selection (our subject) and makes it a new layer in the Layers palette. The marching ants should also disappear.

06 **Paint it black** Cmd/Ctrl-click on the thumbnail of the new layer to reactivate the selection. Go to Edit>Fill and in the dialog box choose Black from the Contents Use list. Keep Mode set to Normal and the Opacity 100%. Hit OK and the subject should go completely black.

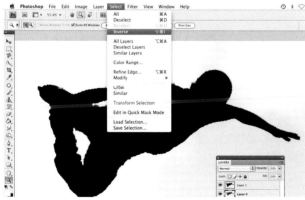

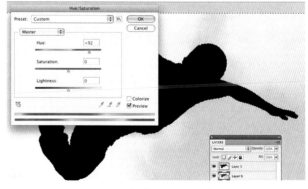

07 **Reach for the sky** Double-click on the background layer containing the sky, and hit OK in the New Layer dialog box to make this editable. With the selection still active, go to Select>Inverse to select the sky.

08 **A touch of pink** For the finishing touch, head to Image>Adjustment>Hue/Saturation. Move the Hue adjustment to the colour of your choice. We've gone for a light pink. Hit OK, and then Cmd/Ctrl+D to remove the selection in order to complete this silhouette effect with an abstract feel.

Create your own optical art

Produce optical illusions using Photoshop's simple tools and quick transformations

Optical art, also known as Op art, uses lines, shapes and symmetry to give an illusion of movement, with the idea of making you disorientated and a little dizzy.

Op art has existed for the best part of half a century, and it made way for a new kind of experimental design. Originally, artists used repetition of geometric shapes hand-crafted for their Op art, but modern forms can now be recreated digitally. In this tutorial we demonstrate how to do just that.

Illusions can be created with colour, shading, or simply with black-and-white shapes, but the resulting image is almost hypnotic. Photoshop makes it extremely easy to turn flat shapes into three-

dimensional illusions. It's a case of designing the initial pattern and then bending it to appear abstract. Photoshop has a variety of Transform tools – including the Distort option, which we've used for our image, making it seem as though you're looking down between two towering skyscrapers.

Learn how to create the chequerboard effect for the side of the buildings using the Actions palette and a couple of commands. This is great for speeding up a potentially lengthy process. Read our side-tip on how to add colour to your illusion if the black-and-white effect doesn't quite do it. But beware… Stare at it too long and you could find yourself feeling a little dizzy!

So let's get stuck in and create some quick Op art in Photoshop.

CREATE MOVEMENT WITH LINES
Use Actions to create a chequerboard effect

01 **Prepare the Layers palette** Open a blank white document, making the dimensions larger than you think you might need, because we'll crop it smaller later on. Create a new layer and go to Edit>Fill. Set the Content Use to Black, and Opacity to 100%. Now hit OK.

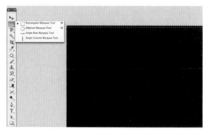

02 **Create a selection** Select the Rectangular Marquee tool and then drag a box over the entire canvas to select all. Using the Down arrow, nudge the selection five times. This determines how large you want the squares to be. Next, go to Select>Inverse.

03 **A new action** Keep the same zoom percentage that you had in Step 2. Go to Window>Actions to open the Actions palette. In the palette click on the Create New Action button. Call it 'Op art' and the Record button will start automatically. Any clicks that you make will now be recorded.

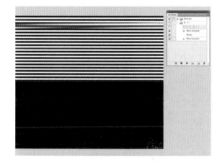

04 **A little more action** Pick the Rectangular Marquee tool and nudge the selection with the Down arrow five times. Hit the Backspace key to erase the black, and repeat. Hit Stop in the Actions palette. Click on the first step and press Play repeatedly to make white lines down the entire image.

05 **Fill it up** Duplicate the layer with the lines. Go to Select>All (Cmd/Ctrl+A). Now go Edit>Transform>Rotate 90 CW to spin the lines to a vertical position. In Edit>Free Transform, stretch the lines to fill the canvas. Hit Cmd/Ctrl+E to merge the line layers.

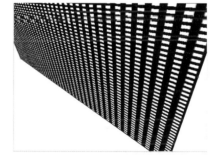

06 **Add some direction** With the Crop tool, select the entire canvas and hit Enter to remove any lines that are off the canvas. Go to Edit>Transform>Distort and manipulate the layer to give it perspective. This is one side of the optical effect.

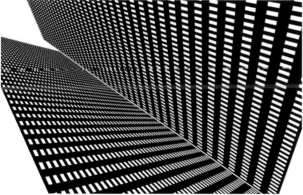

07 **Dizzying heights** When you're happy with the angle and distortion, duplicate the layer. Now go to Edit>Free Transform>Flip Horizontal. Spin this layer around so it mirrors the original layer, leaving a thin gap between them.

08 **Crop to size** Next, use the Distort option in the Transform window again to bend the duplicate so that it looks steeper than the other side. Finally, use the Crop tool, holding down the Shift key, to frame the image into a perfect square and then crop it for a punchy composition.

Pop goes Photoshop

Create an Andy Warhol-inspired work in minutes thanks to blending modes

Andy Warhol's colour- block prints are instantly recognisable. At the time, they were original and eyecatching, and no one had done it before. Now, however, anyone who owns Photoshop can have a go on for themselves with their own portrait shots. You can use any image for this as long as you can crop it into a square shape. We desaturate the image before applying the Cutout filter. When you remove the colour, you need to ensure that there are enough defined areas of black and white for the filter to work well. Finally, we will be creating our final composition of four photos in a square, before adding the funky colours.

Before

QUICK FIX

Top tip: We use Multiply blending mode to create our effect, but you can play with the other options for different effects.

MAKE YOUR PHOTOS 'POP'
Turn images into art

01 **Desaturate and crop** First we need to prep our image for the pop-art effect. First go to Image> Adjustments>Desaturate to remove the colour. Next, choose the Crop tool and fix its Width and Height to the same number so that you have a square – we went for 20 x 20cm. Crop your photo to a perfect square.

02 **Filter effects** Go to Filter>Artistic> Cutout. In the Filter dialog, you can play with the options down the right-hand side – we changed the Number of Levels to 7. Next go to File>New and create a new document that is double the size of the square crop – ours was 40 x 40cm.

03 **Now for the fun bit!** Back on the photo you have been working on, Select All, and copy and paste into the new document. Do this four times and arrange in a square. Add a new layer above each photo layer. Click on the thumbnail for the first photo layer to create a selection. On the new layer above it, Fill with a vibrant colour and set the layer to Multiply blending mode. Repeat for each photo layer.

Colour effects made easy

We'll show you how to add some funky colouring to any photo in minutes

I t's easy to get creative in Photoshop and there are loads of effects out there that you can try to turn your photos into works of art. Luckily, some of these effects don't take more than a few minutes to apply, and this one is a case in point. We're going to add some funky rainbow colours over our portrait image, that will then be blended together nicely with a bit of a blur. You can add as many or as few colours as you want to the image – the sky's the limit!

Top tip: Always use a soft-edged brush or you will find that the colours don't blend together nicely.

Before

QUICK FIX

After

ADDING A WASH OF COLOUR
Let's get creative with our brush

01 **Get ready to colour** Open the image that you want to add the colour effect to. Now, desaturate the image using the Image>Adjustments>Desaturate command. Create a new layer above the photo layer and then pick a large, soft-edged brush from the Brush Options. Now we're ready to begin!

02 **Bright colours** Set your new layer to the Soft Light blending mode in the Layers palette and make sure that the layer is selected. Now pick a nice bright colour and start painting at one end of your image. Colour about a quarter, then switch to another bright colour and repeat until the whole of the image is filled.

03 **Blur it all together** Your image should be a mess of colours. We're going to fix that by using a Blur filter, in this case Gaussian Blur, with a very high Radius so that the different colours bleed together nicely. We have gone for the maximum 250px Radius here. And we're done!

Super-quick paint effects

Use an unusual tool for digital art

If the thought of digital painting appeals to you but you don't want to spend ages tangling with the Brush tool, let the Median filter sort you out. This is part of Photoshop's Noise filter army, but is very handy for smooth detail to give a watercolour effect. It's best used on images that don't rely on loads of detail, and can be just the thing for kick-starting an art project. Once you chuck in a spot of Texturizer filter, you have a convincing effect.

Top tip: The Median filter is also excellent for making backgrounds. Blob a few colours about and then run the Median filter to merge together.

Before

QUICK FIX

After

FILTER ARTWORK
Blur and then bring back detail

01 Instant wash Open up your image and drag its layer down to the New Layer icon to duplicate it. Making sure you are on the duplicate layer, head to the Filter menu, choosing Noise>Median. The window that opens allows you to control how extreme the effect is. The aim is to get a washy look. Somewhere around the 30 mark should do.

02 A touch of detail Now you need to bring back some detail on areas. Pick the Eraser tool and then select a painterly brush. Anything from the Dry Media set works well. Set Opacity to 40% and with a smallish size, lightly brush over areas to reveal the start photo. Be sparing with this – you don't want to revert back to a photo.

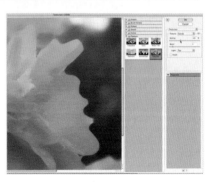

03 Now some texture To finish the art effect, flatten the layers (Layer>Flatten Image), go to the Filter menu and then down to Texture>Texturizer. Pick Canvas from the Texture drop-down menu and then adjust the Scaling and Relief to taste. Click OK and your faux painting is complete!

Quick sketch effects

Transform your photos into swift digital doodles

Unless you are blessed with artistic talent, the chances are that the thought of making a digital drawing from scratch doesn't appeal to you.

But Photoshop has a few tricks up its sleeve to make the task easier. When it comes to making a digital sketch, your new best friends will be the High Pass filter and the Threshold command. While these two are fairly innocuous on their own, when brought together they seek out the outline of a photo and then turn it into a sketch.

Top tip: Don't aim for too much detail in the High Pass stage, otherwise you will end up with heavy black areas.

QUICK FIX

MAKE QUICK SKETCHES
Take one photo and turn it into a drawing

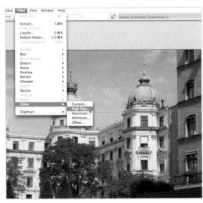

01 **Find the edges** Open up your photo in Photoshop. If your image is lacking contrast, use Levels or Curves to do some boosting. Now go to the Filter menu, down to Other and pick High Pass.

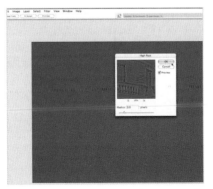

02 **Edit with the slider** Your image will turn a peculiar colour – do not panic! The High Pass filter is for you to seek out the edges of your image. Use the Radius slider to adjust this – the higher you go the thicker the lines will be. Go for something like 3.0.

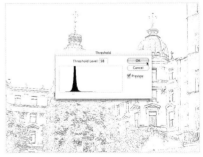

03 **Pencil effect** Click OK to exit the High Pass filter. Next stop is the Image menu and then Adjustments>Threshold. This will turn your image to black and white and once again, there is a slider to edit the effect. In our image, a setting of 58 worked well, and the higher the setting the more intense the effect. Click OK when you are happy.

30 digital painting tips

We reveal the top 30 tips to make your digital painting flow more smoothly

Not many people can lay claim to being able to create real painted masterpieces – so stay clean and don't get out your paints and brushes just **yet.** Why not grab your graphics pen or mouse and open up Photoshop instead?

Possessing real artistic skills can, of course, ultimately boost your paintings. However, you can make things easier for yourself by preparing properly and knowing the basic techniques. Your painting style will improve and you will see your skills flourish with just a little bit of practice.

Digital painting can be just as tricky to master as the 'real thing'. A graphics tablet will be a great boost; these tips can be followed with a mouse, but your brush strokes might be less accurate than you wish and it will be a more frustrating process.

In this feature we reveal 30 top digital painting tips that professional Photoshop users feel are the basis of digital painting. A great image doesn't come together instantly – but learning all the simple elements will point you in the right direction. We'll show you how to start at the beginning by loading your brushes, then how to create your own brushes, and lastly, when you feel ready, how to paint with them.

Putting all these 30 tips together will leave you feeling motivated and inspired to begin painting. So turn the page and get prepared to put our tips to practical use.

Brush types

01

Assorted Brushes
Basic Brushes
Calligraphic Brushes
Drop Shadow Brushes
Dry Media Brushes
Faux Finish Brushes
Natural Brushes 2
Natural Brushes
Special Effect Brushes
Square Brushes
Thick Heavy Brushes
Wet Media Brushes

There are
12 preset
brush packs already in Photoshop. Go to your Brushes palette and click on the small black arrow at the top right of the palette. At the bottom of the list you will find the brush sets. To load one of the sets, simply click it. If you want to add these brushes to the ones already in your palette, click Append when the Option box appears. Now the brushes are loaded and the thumbnails are visible.

The most useful painting brushes:

Wet Media: Oil brush

Dry Media: Pastel brush

Natural Media: Stipple brush

Basic brushes: Soft/hard-edged

Brushes palette

02 If this palette is not already showing, go to Window> Brushes (or F5). This is where all of your brush qualities are determined. We have broken the palette down for quick referencing…

Brush Presets Where your brushes are displayed with a line example drawn.

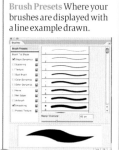

1

Other options In the bottom half of the Brushes palette you can select other option styles to add to your brush, including Noise, Wet Edges, Airbrush, Smoothing and Protect Texture. Some are suited to certain brush styles, but it's all about experimenting.

2

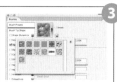

3

Texture You can add texture to your brush when painting here. Select from the drop-down menu or load your own textures. You can also control the blend mode options and the strength of the texture.

Color Dynamics Vary the colour options to your brushes here, allowing the foreground/background colours to alternate mid-flow. Other options include Hue, Saturation and Brightness levels. Note that you can alter the brush controls as well.

4

Dual Brush 7 You can add a second brush to your stroke if needed – great when adding texture to your work.

Other Dynamics 6 Alter the opacity and flow jitters quickly here.

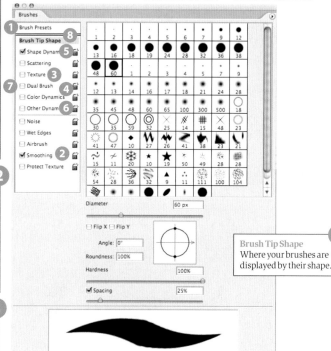

Brush Tip Shape 8 Where your brushes are displayed by their shape.

Shape Dynamics Here you can control your brush size, angle and jitter (which is the variation of the brush).

5

Loading & resetting brushes

03 Loading brushes is simple – just go to your Brushes palette and click on the top right arrow. In the list you will see the Load Brushes option. Click on this and locate the brushes you wish to load, then hit OK. They will be added to your brush library instantly. In this list you can also reset, save and replace brushes.

Shortcuts

04 To increase and decrease brush size, simply press the '[' and ']' keys. To alter opacity press the keyboard numbers, eg for an opacity of 35 hit 3 and 5.

How to paint skin from a photo

05 There are many ways to digitally paint skin. Starting from a sketch and building up gradually is a great choice.

01 Swatches If you don't feel confident about creating skin tones from scratch, open up a photo with good colouring for reference. Select the Brush tool and Opt/Alt-click on a light skin tone. With your colour selected, go to the Swatch palette and click. Repeat for the midtones and shadow tones.

02 Base Double-click your original photo to make it editable and add a new layer above it. Fill this with a midtone skin colour and then lower the opacity so the photo is visible. Select a small brush – we used a Hard Charcoal Edge brush. Sketch out the edges to the image, varying the brush size and opacity as you go.

03 Gradually build it up Create a new layer at the top of the palette. Using the newly filled layer as your medium skin tones, select a shade darker and begin painting the natural darker shades on to your newly added layer. For this example we used a large soft-edged brush at 30% Opacity.

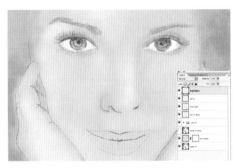

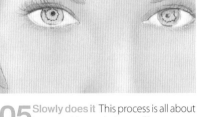

04 Shadows and highlights Select a shade darker and begin on a new layer to paint in the darker face areas. Repeat the process with the highlighted areas. Remember that less is more at this stage – the finishing touches will be added soon.

05 Slowly does it This process is all about low opacities and plenty of layers. Work slowly, altering tones only slightly so that the impact isn't instantly sharp. Make sure you label your layers well, so you can go back easily and edit layers as you paint.

Photo references are perfect for getting started with digital painting. Use them to pick colours or trace around shapes if you can't draw

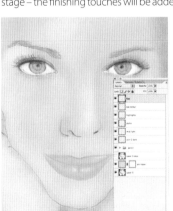

06 Pushing further Once your skin is complete, add a mask to your first filled-in base layer. See tip 9 for mask help if unsure. Paint away on the mask the unwanted areas of colour in the hair, eyes and lips. Use the same gradual technique to add eye and lip colour.

Opacity

06 Use your brush at a low opacity when painting, either on one layer or building up your image slowly layer by layer. Painting with this technique will mean you won't overwork your image too quickly and the effect is more natural. You would paint like this with real paints, so the technique should still be applied in Photoshop.

10%
20%
30%
40%
50%
60%
70%
80%
90%
100%

Create swatches

07 If you want to save colour swatches while painting, simply have the selected colour in your foreground/background (side toolbar), and hover over the Swatch palette and click. Name your swatches for ease of reference if saving a selection.

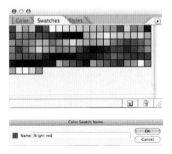

> "This process is all about low opacities and plenty of layers. Work slowly, altering tones only slightly so that the impact isn't instantly sharp"

How to paint foliage

08 Tree embellishments can be created by using a selection of the Stipple brushes found in the Photoshop presets or by making your own custom brushes.

01 Use custom brushes Tip 30 shows you how to make and save your custom brushes, but here's how to use them well. This technique is all about patience and building up with different brush sizes and colours. Set up your canvas and get the bare tree you want to work on ready.

02 Back to basics To create a basic leaf texture, start by selecting two nice leaf colours in the side toolbar. Open the Brushes palette and pick a basic Watercolor brush, then go to Color Dynamics, set it to Pen Pressure and Foreground/ Background Jitter to 50%.

03 A leafy pattern Go to Texture and at the top right arrow select Nature Patterns>Ivy Leaves. Now go to the Shape Dynamics category and select Pen Pressure for all and increase Minimum Diameter to 60%. Lastly, in Brush Tip Shape alter Angle to around 60 degrees.

04 The natural look Go to Edit>Define Brush Preset and save. Now, on your bare tree paint with the blend mode set to Multiply. Keep altering the brush size and angle so that the leaves look natural.

Masks

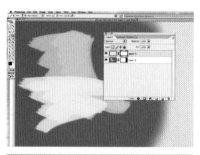

09 When painting, we have all at some time made changes to our work but then changed our mind when it's too late; this is where masks are invaluable. They allow you to easily make non-destructive changes to your artwork.

To add a mask simply go to the foot of the Layers palette and press the Layer Mask icon. A new thumbnail will appear next to your chosen layer.

Set your foreground/background colours to black/white in the side toolbar (quick key 'D'). To erase a section, click the mask thumbnail, select the Brush tool and paint over the area you wish to erase. To paint back into the area, simply press X to switch the foreground and background colours. Now, with white selected, the deleted area will reappear. Remember, it's black to delete and white to bring back.

Dodge and Burn tools

10 These are excellent tools for adding shadows and highlights to your digital artwork. They are especially great on top of a painting with texture, as they bring the richness out.

The tools work like the Brush tool – which makes them nice and simple to use. Keep the strength at a low percentage when using, and build up slowly so you don't overwork your image.

In the top toolbar you can select to alter Midtone, Highlights and Shadows. Stick to the Midtone option for most work to alter all tones.

Before

After

Pen pressure

11 In the Brushes palette all the brush settings give you options to set the tool to Pen Pressure. When using a tablet you need to alter these for the best results – it makes the pen even more magical to work with.

Creating vignettes

12 Most paintings are nicely finished off with a vignette. Choose a large soft-edged brush at a low opacity. Opt/Alt-click a dark area of your image and add some black. Set your brush to Multiply and on a new layer paint over the corners in a curved motion.

Building up texture

13 Creating convincing oil paintings requires a nice thick paint effect. For a great texture brush pick the brush with Thick Flow Medium Tip from the Wet Media brushes set. In the Brushes palette go to Texture and click on the swatches, then choose Weave. Go to the Other Dynamics option and set Opacity Control to Pen Pressure if using a tablet. In the Shape Dynamics section increase the Minimum Size to 100%. The last effect in this palette is in the Brush Tip Shape category. For the Brush Roundness enter 50%, and an Angle between 20-40 is enough.

These settings will create a nice textured brush, but if this is still not enough for your painting needs then add a Bevel and Emboss effect. At the base of the Layers palette go to the Add a Layer Style option and pick Bevel and Emboss. For Style select an Inner Bevel and a Smooth Technique. Keep the Depth low for a natural effect and the Size and Soften options to 0 pixels. Apply these techniques to a thick painted image for a strong textured effect.

In the Layer Styles dialog you can add a Bevel and Emboss effect, which will add to the strong textured look of your image

Layers palette

14 When digitally painting you will end up with tons of layers. To keep order in what can easily become chaos, label each layer. If working on a massive image such as a face, try to group areas of your painting – hair, face, lips, etc. To group layers Cmd/Ctrl-click on each layer you wish to group and then press Cmd/Ctrl+G.

> "These settings will create a nice textured brush, but if this is still not enough for your painting needs then add a Bevel and Emboss effect"

Retouching directly onto photos

Before *After*

15 Use a soft-edged brush at a low opacity to produce some dramatic results

01 Whiten up Begin by making a duplicate of your background layer (double-click to make it editable then drag over the Create New Layer icon). Select a soft brush set to Multiply and 20% Opacity. Use white paint over the teeth and eyes.

02 Digital makeover Create a new layer and select a light skin tone, using the following settings: Cyan: 0%, Magenta: 6%, Yellow: 12%, Black: 0%. On your new layer paint over the model's face. Build up a few layers at low opacity.

03 Finishing touches Keep building up on new layers, darkening the colour tones so the image remains natural. Don't forget to brighten the lips, and perhaps even add some colour to the eyelids and irises.

Tracing a photo

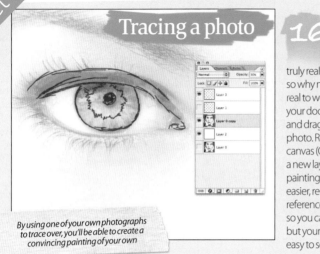

By using one of your own photographs to trace over, you'll be able to create a convincing painting of your own

16 Most of us can only dream about painting something truly realistic from scratch, so why not use something real to work from? Create your document to paint on and drag in your reference photo. Resize it to fit your new canvas (Cmd/Ctrl+T) then add a new layer on top to begin painting on. To make painting easier, reduce Opacity in your reference photo to about 50%, so you can still see the image but your new artwork will be easy to see as it develops.

Dpi

17 Always remember when creating a new canvas to make it as large as possible and always at 300dpi or higher. You can downsize, but you will be disappointed if your masterpiece becomes pixelated when the size is increased.

Quick hair/fur cheat

18 To add the final touches to your painted hair or fur, use the Smudge and Blur tools for natural-looking effects.

Select the Smudge tool, and in the top toolbar choose a small brush between 1-5 pixels and set the Strength to 90%. Simply drag a section of hair or fur outwards. Vary the brush size so you get a convincing selection of fly-away hairs.

To finish this effect off, use the Blur tool at a low opacity and simply paint over a few of the newly appeared hairs.

This is an effective cheat not only in paintings but on photos and cutouts too. Just try not to overwork the image – keep it natural.

Highlighting

19 A really good way to finish an image is by adding some highlights. Just add a lighter tone where needed. Along the bridge of the nose and forehead in portrait images can add enough impact.

Use photos as references; try taking your own photos with different light settings to find out where light naturally falls.

"Try taking your own photographs with different light settings to find out where light naturally falls"

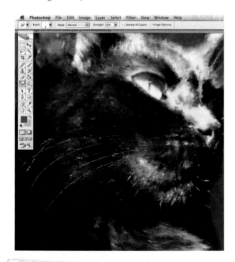

The Smudge and Blur tools can create a wonderfully natural-looking final touch to hair or fur

Creating sea and spray

20 Paint beautiful seas easily with a simple technique

01 Set up Set up a new canvas and fill it with an ocean base colour – here we used C:69, M:13, Y:7 and K:0. Alter this to suit your project. To create great spray, an object like rocks or a boat will be needed.

02 Build up your scene Create a new layer under your rocks and select a lighter blue to start with. Select a large soft-edged brush, set it to Multiply in the top toolbar, with Flow at 70%. Lower Opacity to around 30% to start with and begin painting in some water swirls.

Texture

21 The preset Photoshop textures often look too fake. Adding a nice scanned or bought texture and placing it underneath or on top of your painting can add true realism.

When you have placed the texture onto your artwork, experiment with the different layer blend options and opacity levels. The texture that we used here is an old sheet of paper set to Linear Burn and 45% Opacity. This is a strong example of what effects can be achieved – have fun and be bold.

"Vary the blue shades to bring in the lights and darks of the water, and use different flow and opacity values in order to keep the colours subtle"

03 Water treatments Continue to build up your water gradually, always on new layers. Vary the blue shades to bring in the lights and darks of the water, and use different flow and opacity values to keep the colours subtle. Use photos for reference if you're struggling to visualise.

04 Spray time Select the Dry Brush Tip brush. Lower Flow to 30%, use Normal blend mode and vary the opacity to get the effect. Paint with a dotted motion and keep altering the brush size to build up gradually.

See your chosen brush

22 To be able to see your brush size when painting, go to Photoshop>Preferences> Display and Cursors. Set your cursor as in the screenshot.

Use the Display and Cursors option in Photoshop's Preferences to alter the brush icon you see

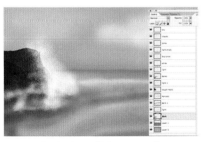

05 Finishing off the spray Revert to the soft-edged brush, select white, and with a low opacity paint around the edges of the spray to add some blur. Finally, select a harder-edged brush, darker blue and Multiply blend mode.

06 Rounding off On a new layer draw a straight line (hold Shift) along the horizon. Select a softer, small brush and blend in with a lighter blue so the line isn't too harsh. This will separate the sky and sea. Finish off with your own embellishments.

Blend modes

23 When painting in different mediums, try experimenting with the layer blending modes. All 23 options can be found in a drop-down menu at the top of the Layers palette. These effects can be applied to a whole layer or to individual brushes as you paint. If you like the effect but not over the whole of your image, use masks to erase some areas – see tip 9. Here are a few examples…

Multiply The most useful blend mode, especially when adding textures to artwork. It multiplies layers' colours to increase dark tones.

Color Burn This blend mode darkens your image using the content of the top layer – great for a colour boost in this example.

Color Dodge This one works best when a mask is applied to the layer. Not a great overall effect, but nice for creating depth where needed. Color Dodge lightens an image.

Overlay Another great blend mode to use when applying a texture, it combines the Screen (lightens) and Multiply (darkens) effects to give a more subtle appearance.

Create straight lines

24 Creating a straight, precise line when painting couldn't be simpler – just hold down Shift while drawing your stroke and it'll conform to straight lines.

Eraser tool painting

25 You can always try reverse painting if you're bored with the more traditional techniques. Why not start with a dark canvas and work back into it with the Eraser tool? You can set it up just as you would a brush, and it's a fun twist.

Want to try something new? Reverse the order for some interesting results!

Colour and lighting tweaks

26 Colour balance and lighting are just as important at the end of a digital painting as they are when working on photo projects.

There are many different ways to alter these factors – the most useful and easy to use being the Levels tool. This can be applied directly to an individual layer, Image>Adjustments>Levels, or as an adjustment layer. For this option go to the base of the Layers palette and select from the Adjustment Layer menu options, Levels.

A new layer will appear which can be moved anywhere in the Layers palette. In the dialog box which has opened, experiment with moving the sliders left and right, or if you want to target specific colours select one from the drop-down menu.

In the Adjustment menu list are some other great editing features. Try them all out and find the ones that fit your needs best.

Before

After

Top brush downloads

There are many great sites where you can download free Photoshop brushes. Here are our top five inspiring sites…

Brusheezy
brusheezy.com
A great, clean, inspiring site for brush downloads. Easy to navigate and the brush selection is extensive.

myphotoshopbrushes.com
myphotoshopbrushes.com
Great for brushes, especially the blood splatter ones. Also good for shapes, gradients and patterns.

Brush King
brushking.eu
Some of the same brushes as the previous site, but some other great stuff is found on here too!

PSBrushes
psbrushes.net
Not a good site aesthetically speaking, but don't be put off – there are some gems to be found here.

Get Brushes.com
getbrushes.com
An easy-to-navigate site which is quick with good content and looks good as well. Definitely worth a look!

Lock Transparent Pixels

This is a great tip to make sure you paint within the lines or only on a set area of a layer.

Click on the layer you wish to keep neat and tidy, then at the top of the Layers palette click on the Lock Transparent Pixels button and a lock icon will appear on your layer.

You can now only paint within the constraints of this layer. To unlock it, simply press the button again.

This is very useful when painting precise areas such as faces, lips and hair.

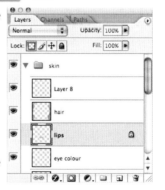

Research your colour palette

If painting in a particular artistic period, remember to pick your brush correctly and also your colours. You don't want to ruin a lovely Art Nouveau piece with garish Pop Art colour! There are many sites to research from, including wikipedia.co.uk. Just spending a few minutes will help your image to develop well.

Custom brushes

Custom brushes can be used for many purposes. Here our example is hair, but all custom brushes are created in the same way. Select a small hard-edged brush and draw a few lines that could resemble hair. Go to Edit>Define Brush Preset and name your brush. You can now use your newly created brush to paint as desired.

This is such a handy technique when creating images from scratch. Just create a simple pattern, for example a strand of hair or a leaf, and then imagine it being repeated.

 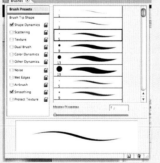 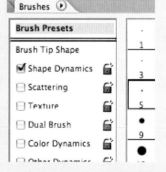

Custom brushes are very versatile, and one of their many purposes is to create a pattern that can be repeated, eg hair or leaves

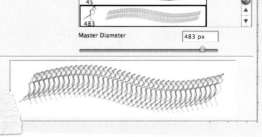

Work faster

Tailor Photoshop to suit your needs and learn how you can make common tasks automated and faster

Learn your shortcuts to navigate Photoshop's tools quicker

152

"Photoshop actions exist to make time-consuming tasks faster"

Top tip: Staying organised with your Photoshop projects will mean that you can always find what you're looking for. Use layer colours and groups to manage big files.

Create droplets to perform common tasks in batch

Let Photoshop do the hard work for you!

136

144

151

Work with multiple
filters for
better effects

138

MacBook Pro

Make sure you know
which layer does what

Understand actions

Get to grips with Photoshop's technical side and learn how this great feature allows you to apply effects over and over

Improving Photoshop's rate of fire, an action is the perfect solution for a busy workflow and takes the hassle out of repeating effects and techniques.

Actions are used to save your favourite effects so you don't need to remember the settings used each time. Actions are addictive, and while you may have used the odd preset action now and then, the addiction only truly begins when you create your own.

Here we've explored the Actions palette and how you can make the most out of using this feature, as well as giving you a step-by-step on how to create your own action from scratch. A new action can be made to do anything, whether that's changing image resolution, saving your artwork as a certain file type or applying a blending mode or layer style. Techniques and adjustments can even be applied all at once to completely overhaul an image in your ultimate action.

Actions exist to make time-consuming tasks faster. For example, if you were looking to create a copyright symbol for applying to a collection of images. As the potential for repetition is high, you should consider using an action to save the steps you take the first time round. After then, it's a case of hitting Play to simply repeat those exact same steps for another image with no extra effort. If you turn to page 146, you'll find out how actions are used in the Batch command.

Editing a custom action
Stopping and starting with ease

So you've created your action but it didn't turn out how you expected it to and you're not happy with the result. Thankfully, you can edit an action and then record from the last command stored to make sure it's perfect every time

01 **A film grain effect** For an action that gives a cool, film grain look to your image, hit record then duplicate the main layer and apply the Add Noise filter with Amount 20%. Change the duplicated layer's blending mode to Soft Light.

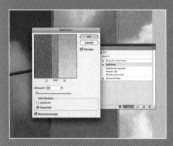

02 **Make action adjustments** The Add Noise filter may look too harsh, in which case delete the duplicated layer. You can then edit the level of noise by double-clicking on the command in the Actions palette. Adjust the Amount to 10%.

03 **Test the adjustment** Go back to the top of the action and hit Play to test out the results. Click on the action's folder to activate the Save Action option in the palette's drop-down menu. Store the effect on your computer for later use.

The Actions palette
The command centre for actions

Actions have their own palette, to record, play and manage commands. The palette lists all your current commands for quick access and each step in a command is visible and editable. Using the drop-down menu at the top of the palette, you can pick from a number of presets. Actions are grouped into sets and have the quality of being editable at any point, meaning any problems with a command can be fixed and replayed. Once an action is set up, you can apply it as many times as you like. They are shortcuts that save you many minutes otherwise spent clicking through menus.

Using presets
A few examples of what can be done

To kick things off, the Actions palette comes loaded with artistic presets to try on your artwork. They're categorised into sets, which include Production, Image Effects, Frames and Text Effects. Simply select one of these and the commands will load into the Actions palette ready for you to use. All that's needed is to hit the Play button at the base of the palette and watch the action take place. Some actions require you to make changes to the adjustment specific to your image. These stop commands can be removed by toggling the small icon next to the command in the Actions palette.

The palette Actions are controlled from within the palette with the Play, Record, Stop and New Action buttons at its base. Actions are listed in the order they'll play, which can also be edited at any point.

Recording your own Hit the Record button to begin your own action. Every click of the mouse is stored inside the palette, but can be deleted and re-recorded at any point.

Controlling actions You can decide how an action responds at each command, whether you want to stop at a particular point or make an adjustment specific to an image. The speed of an action can be altered too for more control over what's going on.

Before

After

The results The image here has been improved using Saturation, Contrast and Sharpening adjustments. The action is now ready for use on other dull and flat images, without having to go through each adjustment.

Organising actions
Loading and staying on top of your actions

New actions can be loaded into the palette using the drop-down menu by clicking on Load Actions. These could either be ones downloaded from the web or actions of your own that you have saved onto the computer. Once loaded into the palette, actions can be moved around in an order that best suits your workflow. They can be reset, renamed, duplicated or even replaced, and this adaptable nature gives you lots of room to play around and organise the palette's layout. The key to a great Actions palette is naming and grouping them together for speed and efficiency.

Playback options
Adjusting the speed of an action

The Actions palette has three options for changing the speed of an action. These are: Accelerated, where the Action will run through an entire command without stopping or showing the effects as they happen; Step by Step, which makes sure each command in the action is finished before it moves to the next one; and Pause For, where you can set the time in seconds between each command. Adjusting the speed of an action will make sure steps perform correctly.

SET UP THE ACTION TO BOOST COLOUR, CONTRAST & SHARPNESS
How a lengthy process can be reduced to just seconds for retouching photos

01 Create a new action Open the first underexposed file that you want to edit. Next, open up the Actions palette (Window>Actions) and click on the Create New Set button. Name the set Photo Retouches.

02 Name the action Click on the Create New Action button in the Actions palette. In the pop-up box, name this action Colour, Contrast, Sharpen. Under the Function Key, set to None and then hit Record to begin creating your action.

03 We're rolling! The red Record button should be highlighted in the palette, which means the action is recording our ever click. The first command is to drag the Background layer onto the Create New button in the Layers palette to duplicate, then this will be how the action always starts.

04 Boost colours To enhance the saturation of the image, go to Image>Adjustments>Hue/Saturation, and move the Saturation slider to +30. Hit OK, and the command should record and show up in your Actions palette.

05 Improve contrast For the next command in the action, go to Image>Adjustments>Brightness/Contrast, and increase Contrast to +30. This should bring more life to highlights and shadows. If you make a mistake, simply stop the action, delete the command, and record again.

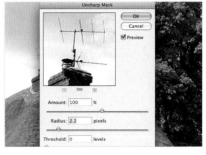

06 Improve sharpness To boost the sharpness of the image, go to Filter>Sharpen>Unsharp Mask. Enter 100% for Amount, 2.2px for Radius and set Threshold to 0. Hit OK to apply the sharpening, and hit Stop in the palette to complete the action.

Automate actions
More auto-pilot commands

Actions are an integral part of Photoshop's Automate commands (found under File>Automate). Using actions will speed up processes that would otherwise take many editing hours. The Batch command can be set up using a custom or preset action assigned to it, and is a fast way to edit a folder of images in one go. To set one up, go to the Batch menu and

select the desired action under Play. Select the folder you want to use and choose the destination, whether that's a specific folder or simply to stay open in Photoshop once the action has been applied. Check the final steps in this article to find out how to apply a droplet.

Action shortcuts
A quicker way to apply actions

Actions are time-savers of postproduction, but you can speed up their already fast reactions using shortcuts officially known as Function Keys. Function Keys use F1-15, and allow you to apply an action at the press of a button. There

are two ways to set up a Function Key. The first is to choose one when you create a new action. In the New Action window simply select the desired key. The second method is to apply a function after an action is made, using the Action Options menu (from inside the Actions palette).

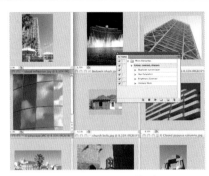

07 **Test and improve** Try the action on a range of images to see the results. Pressing Play will run the commands instantly and you can adjust any settings by double-clicking on the command, which opens the adjustment for you to alter.

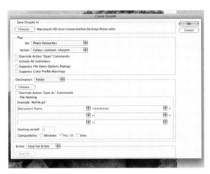

08 **Create a droplet** Go to File>Automate>Create Droplet, and under Choose, select your computer's desktop to save the droplet on. Once the droplet is created, it lets you drag images onto its icon to apply the action.

09 **Set up commands** In the Droplet menu, under Play, change Set to the action you just made – Photo Retouches. The Action area should show Colour, Contrast, Sharpen, and make sure the four boxes underneath Play are all unchecked.

10 **Change destination** Under Destination, change its setting to None as we want to keep the images open after applying the action. This will hide the remaining options under File Naming. Keep Errors set to Stop for Errors then hit OK to complete your droplet.

11 **Locate the droplet** A new droplet icon should now be on your desktop screen as a blue arrow. To use the action applied to the droplet, highlight a bunch of images then drag and drop them onto the icon to load in Photoshop.

12 **Changing opacities** Go through your images in Photoshop and they should have the adjustments applied onto a duplicate layer. If the adjustment is too strong on an image, lower the opacity of the top layer in the Layers palette.

Action resources
Download free actions

There are many resources online for downloading free actions to try out on your artwork. Websites such as **www.visual-blast.com**, **www.hongkiat.com** and **http://designreviver.com** offer various effects as actions, all ready to launch into Photoshop. Once they've been downloaded, go into the Action palette's drop-down menu and click on the Load Actions button. Sourced from all over the web, these sites have many different actions for experimenting with to load your palette to the brim with interesting effects. It's a case of filing them away to use at the right moment.

Exchange actions
Get feedback on your custom actions

Why not create actions to share with fellow artists? Save your favourite actions onto your computer via the Actions palette, and then let fellow artists try them out on their images to see what they think. If you have your own website or blog, upload them and allow other users to download and try them out. It's one of the best ways to learn Photoshop inside and out, and you'll be able to speed up your workflow by becoming a master of actions.

Making droplets

Improve your workflow with this well-kept secret – droplets

The Droplets function is another of Photoshop's shortcuts that can easily go unnoticed. Hidden away under File>Automate>Create Droplet, this handy little tool is a real time-saver when it comes to batch processing your images.

First things first – you need to familiarise yourself with the Actions palette to be in with a chance of understanding the Droplets command. Without any actions set up in Photoshop there's no need to make a droplet. A droplet is a small icon that you can store anywhere on your computer: on your desktop or in a folder. They contain a certain action from within Photoshop, which you can invent yourself or, if preferred, use a preset action.

Droplets are used by dragging an individual image or a folder of multiple images onto its icon. It will then open the image(s) in Photoshop and automatically apply the action that was assigned to it.

Thankfully, Photoshop has made things even easier. There are already actions set up in the Actions palette, with a choice of anything from applying textures to fixing a border to an image. You can use an action without the aid of a droplet by clicking on a small Play button in its palette when an image is open.

If you're a hard working Photoshopper, you'll find that collecting individual droplets on your computer – and having all your favourite actions ready at your disposal – will be a great help.

Droplets galore

Get to know the Actions palette (reached via the Window menu), and you can start making your own collection of droplets. Here's a guide to start you off

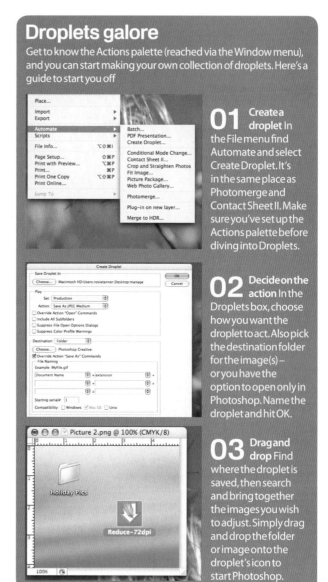

01 Create a droplet In the File menu find Automate and select Create Droplet. It's in the same place as Photomerge and Contact Sheet II. Make sure you've set up the Actions palette before diving into Droplets.

02 Decide on the action In the Droplets box, choose how you want the droplet to act. Also pick the destination folder for the image(s) – or you have the option to open only in Photoshop. Name the droplet and hit OK.

03 Drag and drop Find where the droplet is saved, then search and bring together the images you wish to adjust. Simply drag and drop the folder or image onto the droplet's icon to start Photoshop.

Fast image effects
Sepia toning with ease

Not bad at all – the Sepia action looks very convincing, and it really couldn't be easier. Just make a droplet from File> Automate>Create Droplet, and choose the Sepia Tone preset from the Actions list. You can find the effect under Image Effects>Sepia Toning. You'll see two options for making a sepia tone, Greyscale or Layer, but we chose the Layer option for this image. When the droplet is created it will save in a specified location (default is your desktop). Using the Droplet icon, just drag and drop an image onto it, then sit back and watch Photoshop do it all for you!

Essential processes
A smarter Smart Sharpen

Once you've mastered the preset actions, you can venture to create your own personalised actions. Here, we've made a Smart Sharpen action for a quick post-production necessity. This will work great with a folder full of images, as you can drag a whole folder onto a droplet's icon. Photoshop will load automatically, applying the Smart Sharpen to all images inside. It's a good idea to tick the Include All Subfolders box in the Droplets dialog box, as this will make sure all the images in all folders will be included when dragged onto its icon.

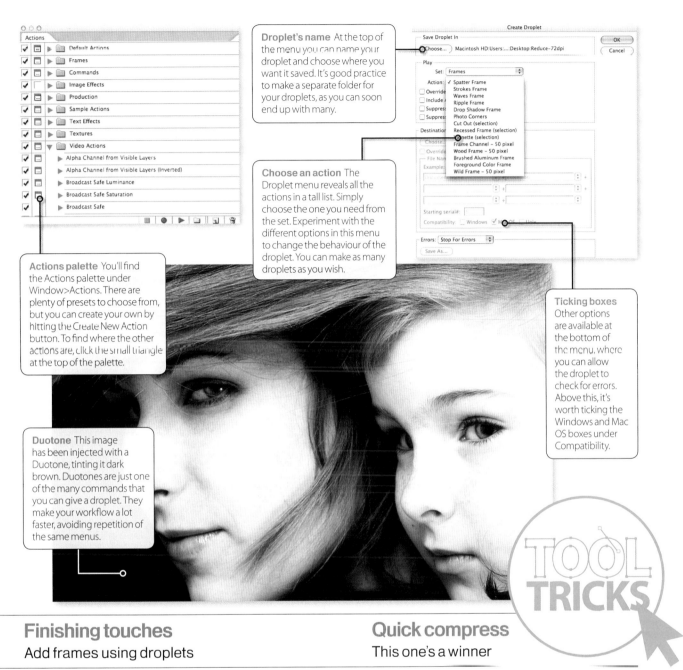

Droplet's name At the top of the menu you can name your droplet and choose where you want it saved. It's good practice to make a separate folder for your droplets, as you can soon end up with many.

Choose an action The Droplet menu reveals all the actions in a tall list. Simply choose the one you need from the set. Experiment with the different options in this menu to change the behaviour of the droplet. You can make as many droplets as you wish.

Actions palette You'll find the Actions palette under Window>Actions. There are plenty of presets to choose from, but you can create your own by hitting the Create New Action button. To find where the other actions are, click the small triangle at the top of the palette.

Ticking boxes Other options are available at the bottom of the menu, where you can allow the droplet to check for errors. Above this, it's worth ticking the Windows and Mac OS boxes under Compatibility.

Duotone This image has been injected with a Duotone, tinting it dark brown. Duotones are just one of the many commands that you can give a droplet. They make your workflow a lot faster, avoiding repetition of the same menus.

Finishing touches
Add frames using droplets

Among the many presets available in the Actions palette, there are a good selection of frames to choose from. Depending on your image, some frames will look plain ugly, but with this image we've chosen a subtle Spatter frame as a finishing touch. When creating your droplets, it's best to name each one with the command that's been assigned. You can customise the action to change the colours or style of the frame, but this must be done before making it a droplet.

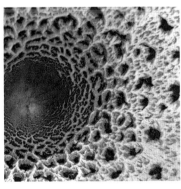

Quick compress
This one's a winner

A droplet for converting a folder of images down to a lower resolution is bound to save precious time. This action is found under Production> Save As JPEG Medium. If Medium is too large, you can alter the compression size by double-clicking on the action in the palette. When creating

the droplet for this command, choose a folder for it to save the images into. Alternatively, you can create a separate droplet for reducing the resolution only, but remember to make the action first!

TOOL TRICKS

Set up the action The Batch menu starts off with 'Play', where you have to input the action you want to carry out on your images. This action is made using the Actions palette. The next step is to choose the folder with the image in it.

Automate workflow

Let Photoshop do the hard work for you with the Automate commands

The appealing nature of Photoshop is the amount of free rein you're given, with many tools at your disposal. But when it comes to creating certain effects on many images at once, this can be tedious, time-consuming and just plain hassle. That's where Automate comes into play.

The Automate function (File>Automate) contains quite a number of effects and commands, and they need little effort to apply. Some of the Automate commands work in conjunction with the Actions palette, and this requires you to set up an action beforehand.

One such command that uses an action is the Batch command. Find out below what this can do for your workflow and how it can reduce the amount of time it takes for you to edit a group of images at once. The main advantage of using the Automate commands for undergoing image-editing tasks is the speed at which they work. Imagine having a folder with 100 images in it and they all need one adjustment made – for example a boost of saturation. Doing this separately for each one would be enough to drive anyone close to insanity, but the Batch Processing command can deal with the task at breakneck speed.

And you'll find there's a lot more to Automate than batch processing. You can convert multiple exposures of one shot to an HDR image, create a droplet and also create a panorama image.

Batch processing
Apply an effect to multiple images

Batch processing applies a certain Action command to a folder of images all in one hit. The requirement for batch processing images is that the action needs to be made beforehand. This could be changing resolution, from RGB to CMYK, or for applying an effect to a group of images. Whatever it is you're looking to do with your images, using Batch is an easy way to cut out repeating the same command 20, 30 or 40 times in a row – Photoshop does the hard work for you. In the Batch menu you can define the action you want to apply, and whether it's to all opened images or from a stored folder. Adobe Bridge can also be linked to the Batch command.

Create Droplet
The helpful little icon

Similar to the Batch command under Automate, droplets let you drag a folder of images onto the Droplet icon on your desktop to apply a specified command. Droplets work with actions too, and this has to be set up before creating a droplet. You can choose where the Droplet command sits on your computer, and they can even operate before PS is opened. Simply by dragging a folder of images onto a droplet, PS loads up and applies the assigned command to the images inside. Why not create loads of droplets, each with its own Action command, to speed your workflow?

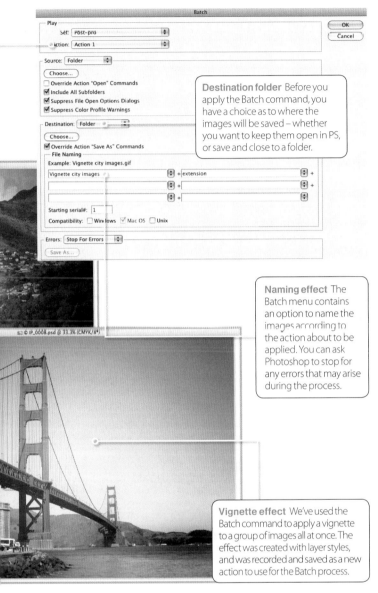

Destination folder Before you apply the Batch command, you have a choice as to where the images will be saved – whether you want to keep them open in PS, or save and close to a folder.

Naming effect The Batch menu contains an option to name the images according to the action about to be applied. You can ask Photoshop to stop for any errors that may arise during the process.

Vignette effect We've used the Batch command to apply a vignette to a group of images all at once. The effect was created with layer styles, and was recorded and saved as a new action to use for the Batch process.

Creating a panorama

Enjoy expansive vistas with Photoshop's Photomerge function. You can stitch together a sequence of images for a fantastic effect

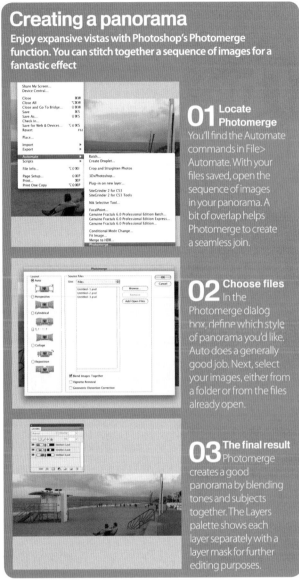

01 Locate Photomerge
You'll find the Automate commands in File> Automate. With your files saved, open the sequence of images in your panorama. A bit of overlap helps Photomerge to create a seamless join.

02 Choose files
In the Photomerge dialog box, define which style of panorama you'd like. Auto does a generally good job. Next, select your images, either from a folder or from the files already open.

03 The final result
Photomerge creates a good panorama by blending tones and subjects together. The Layers palette shows each layer separately with a layer mask for further editing purposes.

Photomerge
Create panoramas and composites

The Photomerge option has come a long way in terms of its ability to successfully 'stitch' images together, and in CS5 the results look excellent. The key behind creating a perfect stitch is in the shooting process. Make sure there is plenty of overlap and that the angle of one image to the next is similar – this makes it easier for Photoshop to examine and align each image. Composites can take the form of different shapes such as cylindrical, spherical, perspective, collage and reposition. Other options include vignette removal and distortion correction for better results.

HDR merging
Use multiple exposures and Automate

Photoshop's Automate also houses the command Merge To HDR (high dynamic range). This combines multiple exposures of one scene to create an HDR image. The important point to remember when constructing your HDR image is to make sure the images are aligned perfectly when shot and that each exposure is different from the last. This makes for a perfect composition with no 'ghosting' of subjects. The command automatically combines the exposures of the images to create a high-contrast and detailed version of your original.

The Preset Manager

Let this handy feature help you streamline the way you work by customising Photoshop's default palette settings

The Preset Manager is the first point of call for those who want to become more organised when working in Photoshop. It allows you to manage all of your brushes, preset tools, gradients, swatches, patterns, custom shapes and contours in one place. This is where you will go to control all of the content in your various presets and those you have created yourself too. The Preset Manager can be found under the Edit menu of Photoshop, and once it is loaded up it is possible to access and organise all of the items in a variety of different libraries. You will initially be working with the Preset Type drop-down menu in the Preset Manager as this is where the kind of tools you are organising are chosen. For example, with Swatches selected in the drop-down menu you can alter the options that will be available to you when working within the Swatches palette. The Preset Manager works in a similar way no matter which Preset Type you are concentrating on. For instance, different collections of brushes or gradients can be added to the current selection that is displayed by making use of the Load button and locating new sets or clicking the arrow in the top right. By using the list that appears you can select the ones you want to be available in your Photoshop palettes.

Create your own brush sets

Use the Preset Manager to organise your brushes into sets. These can be loaded up or added to an existing collection of brushes to access via the Brush tool

01 Create your brushes
The item you want to make into a brush should have a white background. Use the Marquee tool to select the area you want to make into a brush, go to Edit>Define Brush and then name it.

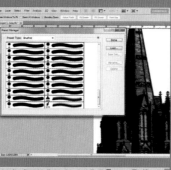

02 Locate the new brushes
Repeat this step to create more brushes. Now choose Edit>Preset Manager to enter the workspace and select Brushes from the Preset Type. Scroll down and your brushes should appear at the bottom.

03 Set saving
Cmd/Ctrl-click each of the brushes you want to save in the Preset Manager. Now click Save Set, choose a location and save it once you have entered a name. Now you can load the new set and add them to existing collections.

Load libraries
Amend or append your default options

The Preset Type that will automatically appear is Brushes. However, you can choose different options using the drop-down menu. The brushes displayed here are those that will be available in the Brushes palette of Photoshop when working with the Brush tool. To change the items that appear in the main area of the Preset Manager (which by default will be the Basic Brushes), click on the arrow in the top right corner and other libraries will appear at the bottom of the list. For example, choose Calligraphy Brushes and you will be asked if you want to replace the current set with this new option. By clicking OK, all of the Calligraphic brushes will appear. If you want to add all of the Calligraphic brushes to the basic set, choose Append instead.

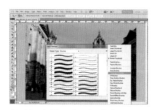

Change the interface
Adjust the way presets are displayed

The Preset Manager can be customised by clicking the arrow in the top right of the window. A selection of display options such as Small Thumbnail and Large List will appear. By choosing one of these options, the items within each of the Preset Types will display in a different way. For example, if you were working with the Swatches list of items, you may prefer to work with a limited visual so you can see just the different shades available. You might need to know each of the Pantone names for your piece, however, in which case it would be better to switch and display the items as a Large List, which will include any additional information.

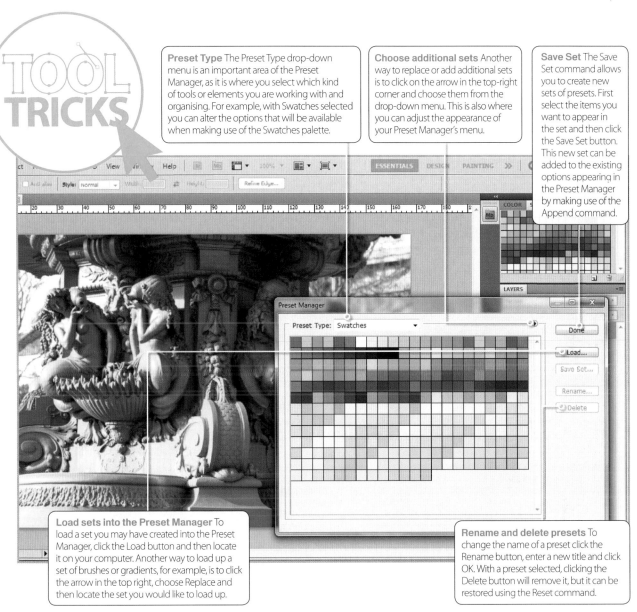

Preset Type The Preset Type drop-down menu is an important area of the Preset Manager, as it is where you select which kind of tools or elements you are working with and organising. For example, with Swatches selected you can alter the options that will be available when making use of the Swatches palette.

Choose additional sets Another way to replace or add additional sets is to click on the arrow in the top-right corner and choose them from the drop-down menu. This is also where you can adjust the appearance of your Preset Manager's menu.

Save Set The Save Set command allows you to create new sets of presets. First select the items you want to appear in the set and then click the Save Set button. This new set can be added to the existing options appearing in the Preset Manager by making use of the Append command.

Load sets into the Preset Manager To load a set you may have created into the Preset Manager, click the Load button and then locate it on your computer. Another way to load up a set of brushes or gradients, for example, is to click the arrow in the top right, choose Replace and then locate the set you would like to load up.

Rename and delete presets To change the name of a preset click the Rename button, enter a new title and click OK. With a preset selected, clicking the Delete button will remove it, but it can be restored using the Reset command.

Save your sets
Customise your brush presets

As well as working with existing presets, you can create your own. For example, if you have created a few brush presets (see our three-step tutorial for how to do this) they will appear in the Preset Manager. But you may want to group these new items into a set of brushes. In the Preset Manager select Brushes

from the Preset Type menu, Cmd/Ctrl-click on the new brushes you had previously made and choose Save Set. Select a location to save the set in and name it. This can now be loaded into an existing collection by clicking Load and locating them.

Load up your saved sets
Expand your resources

To find the new sets you have created within the Preset Manager choose Load and then locate the set of brushes, swatches or gradients in the appropriate location. They will then appear at the bottom of

the selection of brushes that are displayed in the main Preset Manager window. You can also load in the new brush sets created in the Preset Manager when working with the Brush tool. In the top Options bar, open the Brush Preset Picker, click the arrow to the right and choose Load Brushes to locate the brush set.

Work with Tool Presets

You'll never have to set up a tool again by mastering the Tool Presets feature

If you find yourself constantly repeating the steps for setting up a particular tool you use on a regular basis, you'll definitely need to know about time-saving Tool Presets.

A Tool Preset is a saved property of the tool you're using, and it can be recalled at any time. It could be that you prefer the Brush tool to be set up with a specific blending mode, or set to 10% Opacity, or with a certain colour. Or you may be looking to use the Healing Brush tool in a big retouching project and will be needing different settings for different areas of the image and for different subjects.

The Tool Presets feature comes with a palette, and is even available in the Options bar (if you ever wonder what the far left box does, this is it). Nearly every tool in Photoshop can have its own preset. And it doesn't just have to be one; it could be hundreds of presets for one tool, each specifying a different characteristic for that tool. It's an extremely useful time-saver, and is just one of the many methods in which you can speed up the way you use Photoshop.

Load up the palette and explore the existing range of presets, and you can manage them too, to keep what could potentially be a huge collection.

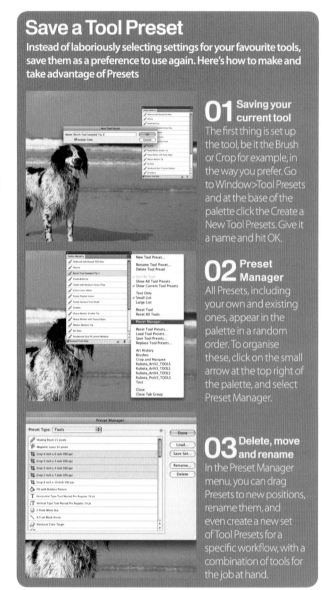

Save a Tool Preset

Instead of laboriously selecting settings for your favourite tools, save them as a preference to use again. Here's how to make and take advantage of Presets

01 Saving your current tool
The first thing is set up the tool, be it the Brush or Crop for example, in the way you prefer. Go to Window>Tool Presets and at the base of the palette click the Create a New Tool Presets. Give it a name and hit OK.

02 Preset Manager
All Presets, including your own and existing ones, appear in the palette in a random order. To organise these, click on the small arrow at the top right of the palette, and select Preset Manager.

03 Delete, move and rename
In the Preset Manager menu, you can drag Presets to new positions, rename them, and even create a new set of Tool Presets for a specific workflow, with a combination of tools for the job at hand.

Make your own
Saving the setup of a tool

The Tool Presets palette is there to make things easier. When you're working on a project, for example a painting using the Brush tool, you may be using one or more different brush shapes with different adjustments that you've chosen to work with. Instead of having to re-set the brush to a different setting each time, which could eat up extra time, you can save different brushes in the Tool Presets palette. From now on, it's just a case of clicking on the preset for the brush and it will change straightaway, so you can spend more time painting and less time in menus. This applies for many other tools in Photoshop, and the list of presets can go on and on.

Manage Tool Presets
Arrange the order to suit your workflow

Tool Presets can be re-arranged using the Preset Manager, found in the drop-down menu in its palette (Window>Tool Presets). In the Preset Manager's dialog box, you can drag a preset to a different position in the list as a way of creating a hierarchy. If you have created a lot of presets, and also use these with existing presets that Photoshop has set up, this would be a good place to start to separate your own from the others. You can also rename and delete presets from here, to keep a tidy palette.

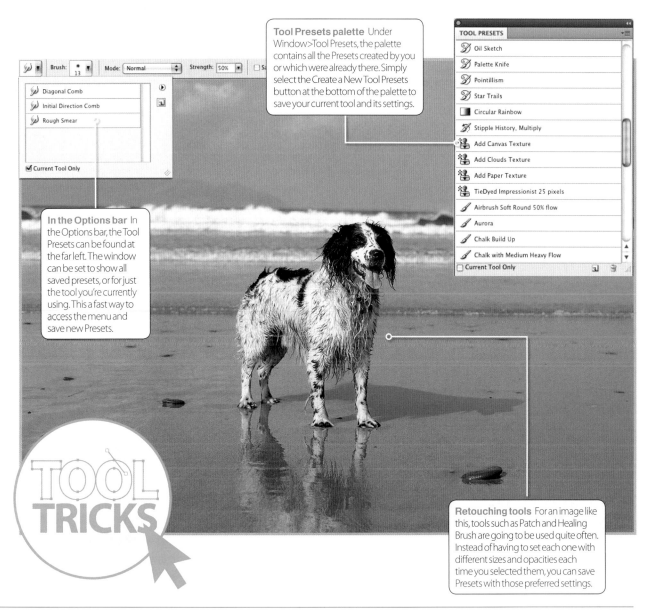

Tool Presets palette Under Window>Tool Presets, the palette contains all the Presets created by you or which were already there. Simply select the Create a New Tool Presets button at the bottom of the palette to save your current tool and its settings.

In the Options bar In the Options bar, the Tool Presets can be found at the far left. The window can be set to show all saved presets, or for just the tool you're currently using. This a fast way to access the menu and save new Presets.

Retouching tools For an image like this, tools such as Patch and Healing Brush are going to be used quite often. Instead of having to set each one with different sizes and opacities each time you selected them, you can save Presets with those preferred settings.

TOOL TRICKS

Saving 'sets'
Make a group of presets for specific jobs

Depending on the job at hand, you may end up using a variety of tools to make adjustments and edits. The Tool Presets palette can be used to create a set of presets for the job, which can then be quickly selected without the need to repeat the set up of the tool each time. To create a set, go to the Tool Presets palette and open the drop-down list of options and select Preset Manager. Highlight the tools you want to group together in the set, then hit Save Set. You can now load and share your presets.

'Current Tool Only' option
Toggle this to view all or only some of the presets

The Tool Presets palette has the option Current Tool Only. With this box selected, only the presets for that tool at hand will show, whether they have been homemade or were already there. Toggle this option to show all the presets which exist. By clicking on a preset, the tool at hand will automatically change to the settings saved. When working with the Tool Presets palette, it's a good idea to keep this option selected as you work to make things easier.

Organise your layers

Discover three quick and easy ways to get your layers looking shipshape

Layers are a fundamental part of using Photoshop, which is why it's so vital to keep them organised and tidy.

In big projects, all those layers can soon mount up and leave you feeling bewildered and confused.

To keep things in order, we have three top steps you can implement to help control those layers. Discover how to colour your layers for instant recognition, tidy them away in a folder, or merge them together without losing any of your editing capabilities. So let's begin…

Top tip: To move a selection of layers up or down the palette, hold Cmd/Ctrl and click the ones you wish to move. They'll link together so you can drag or delete.

THE LAYERED LOOK
Three ways to get your layers organised

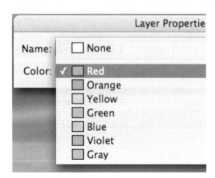

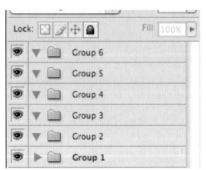

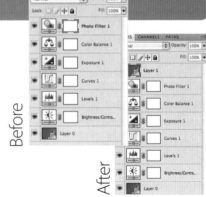

01 **Colour code them** If you like an at-a-glance way of arranging your layers, try this colour coding method. Choose any individual layer and Ctrl/right-click on the eye icon to the left of that layer. A colour list will pop up and you can select your desired hue with a simple click.

02 **Group them in folders** If your Layers palette is getting out of control, it's often a good idea to group similar layers in folders. Do this by simply clicking the folder icon at the bottom of the palette and dragging the desired layers into that folder. Don't forget to name each folder.

03 **Secret Merge technique** To merge all your layers together without losing the flexibility of being able to edit them individually, we have a nifty little trick called Stamp Visible. It's only available through this finger-twisting shortcut: Ctrl+ Alt+Shift+E for PC users and Cmd+ Opt+Shift+E for Mac users.

Increase History states

Don't lose any of your edits – bump up the number of History states and you can undo to your heart's content!

QUICK FIX

We all know the bliss of being able to undo – in fact, wouldn't life be better if we could carry the Undo function into it! But even this technological wonder has its limits, and in the case of Photoshop the limit is measured by the History function.

Open up the History palette (Window>History) and you will see a list of every move you have made in a document. Want to revert back to how your image looked five edits ago? Simply click that state in History and you are right back there.

Photoshop ships with a default number of History states, meaning that if you make more than is set you'll be losing the earlier functions to make way for the new ones. But fear not – there is a way around it…

Top tip: Don't get too carried away with how many history states you set. Too many and you risk making your machine slow down to a crawl.

BUMP UP YOUR HISTORY STATES
Make sure you won't get caught out if you need to return to an early edit

01 **Photoshop CS2 and earlier** Go to the Edit menu (PC) or Photoshop menu (Mac) and scroll down to Preferences. Pick the General option and you'll see a History States area. Simply type in the number you want.

02 **Photoshop CS3 and above** If you are working in CS3 or later, your History states are in a different place. Still open up the Preferences, but instead of General, pick Performance. Type a number or use the slider to set the number of states.

03 **Edit at will** With the new levels of History set, you can make edits safe in the knowledge that you'll be able to return to earlier versions should something go awry. However, please be aware that the more states you have, the more memory-hungry the History will become. If your machine starts to flag, try reducing the number.

The Batch command

Actions are useful things, but how about using an action on multiple images? Enter the marvellous Batch command

If the thought of scripts has you breaking out in a nervous sweat but you're faced with 50 photos all needing the same kind of treatment, don't despair; the world of actions and the Batch command were made for you. Actions are recorded processes that can be applied automatically, but only to one image at a time. The job of the Batch command is to gather up either all open images, or those in a specific folder (it can also process images via Adobe Bridge and Import) and apply a specific action to all of them. The files are then saved to another folder of your choosing. Take, for example, a set of portrait photos that you want to convert to black and white. There's no need to laboriously manually convert each one because you can just run a Batch command to apply a black-white gradient and save a new file, leaving the originals untouched, all in one fell swoop. To access it, simply go to File>Automate>Batch which brings up the Batch dialog. The interesting thing is that actions can be saved in sets, so each set can offer multiple options. Photoshop usually comes with a range of presets, however it only loads the Default Actions set as standard. In this article we'll look at the basics of how to use the Batch command as well as how to add more actions to the list for all your image-editing needs.

Let's go monochrome

The LAB Photo Toner action set comes with CS4 and is great for editing. We used it with a selection of portrait images, but the principle works with any action

01 Load them up
First, load all of your images into Photoshop. Click on the Actions palette, and then the down arrow on the right. Click on Load Actions. Select the 'LAB - Black & White Technique. atn' file and load it on in.

02 Set the parameters
The next step is to go to File>Automate>Batch. Click on the down arrow in the Set box and select the LAB - Black & White Technique action. Now select the Source as Opened Files and the Destination as None.

03 Make adjustments
By default, this action will give your portraits a light sepia effect. As it runs it will prompt to Continue or Stop altogether. Click on Continue and either adjust the saturation or simply click on OK to continue through each.

Load up the effect
Before you can batch, you must have an action

The Batch command will only run the actions that you have loaded, so the first step to making full use of it is to get all the actions that you want loaded up. You can download lots of great ones for free and keep them neatly stored in the folder along side those that come with Photoshop. Ensure any files are unzipped and copy them to the Photoshop>Presets> Actions folder. Then, in Photoshop, click on the Actions palette and then the down arrow in the top right corner. Look down the menu until you find Load Actions. Click on it and navigate to the Actions folder to load them in.

Action options
Understand and customise sets

It's all well and good loading up the Batch command with wild and wonderful actions you've downloaded, but it makes sense to know what it is they are actually going to do. To find out, ensure the action is loaded, then go to the Actions palette and click on the down arrow in front of the action's name. This will list all the processes that are going to be applied. If one element throws up a dialog box in mid-process and you normally just hit return to OK it, you can turn off these individual dialog prompts here. You can also skip individual steps in the action as well – just remove the tick on the left to customise the set to a particular image.

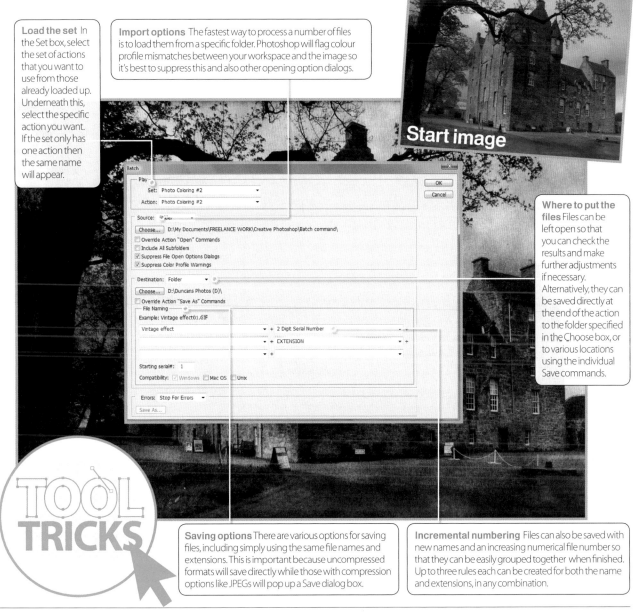

Load the set In the Set box, select the set of actions that you want to use from those already loaded up. Underneath this, select the specific action you want. If the set only has one action then the same name will appear.

Import options The fastest way to process a number of files is to load them from a specific folder. Photoshop will flag colour profile mismatches between your workspace and the image so it's best to suppress this and also other opening option dialogs.

Start image

Where to put the files Files can be left open so that you can check the results and make further adjustments if necessary. Alternatively, they can be saved directly at the end of the action to the folder specified in the Choose box, or to various locations using the individual Save commands.

Saving options There are various options for saving files, including simply using the same file names and extensions. This is important because uncompressed formats will save directly while those with compression options like JPEGs will pop up a Save dialog box.

Incremental numbering Files can also be saved with new names and an increasing numerical file number so that they can be easily grouped together when finished. Up to three rules each can be created for both the name and extensions, in any combination.

Safety first
Manage your actions before saving

If an action has a lot of processing in its set, it can be difficult to tell exactly what the final result is going to be. For that reason, it's worth running an example before you waste memory saving the results. That way you can be sure you're happy with what has been done. The simplest way to check a batch of images is to run the Batch

command on the open files in Photoshop, then check the results and make any adjustments before manually saving. If the Batch prompts to flatten an image before processing the next one, stop that action but then let it continue with the next one, so all the adjustments remain editable.

Simple actions
Add your own to the process

You can create and add your own actions to the sets that are already loaded by recording the process and saving it. Once saved, the Batch command can access your recorded action and use it. If it's something fairly simple where you

know what kind of result it is going to give, there's no need to individually check each file before saving. Instead, in the Destination box enter Save and Close as the option to have it automatically resave the file once the action set has run.

Let's go scripting

Discover the power of Photoshop scripts, without having to learn a new language

Scripts work a lot like actions in that they automatically apply a set of effects to your image. Written in code, they're either in VB Script for Windows, AppleScript for Mac users or JavaScript, which works for both systems. They can perform processes based on conditional logic, meaning they react intuitively to each image. If a script reads a file that's web sized, for example, it might apply a different set of sharpening parameters than it would to an image it identifies as high-res; the scripts apply logic and make changes accordingly.

But who wants to have to learn JavaScript to take advantage of this great feature? Don't worry, you don't have to be a code head to use scripts because there are some supplied with Photoshop itself and there are lots of third party ones, many for free. What you need to do is learn how to install them, how to run a script, understanding the Events Manager and using them automatically.

Scripts first appeared with Photoshop 7 as an optional plug-in and were supplied directly in Photoshop CS. Since then they've been fully integrated so all versions of Photoshop CS can use scripts. The supplied scripts and any that you have installed yourself are contained under File>Scripts, which is also the location of the Scripts Event Manager and the script-based Image Processor.

Scripting in practice

Let's use a script for real and see how it works. We downloaded a script from www.morris-photographics.com called 'black and white variations'

01 Install the script
The script was downloaded and copied to the Scripts folder. It had to be unblocked as described in the tip box. Start Photoshop, load the source image and go to File>Scripts> BW Variations.

02 Script options
This script creates black-and-white effects and here's where you can try different ones. Tick them all. Select a target location for the images when saved and tick Reload Variations so you can directly compare.

03 Compare and delete
Now there are 20 variations to check over. Drag to one side the ones you like, close the ones you don't, and you can compare a couple to see which give the best outright result or platform for further work.

Loading scripts
How to add new ones

There's a handsome supply of scripts available on the web with plenty of freebies. To use them in Photoshop find where the file is, download it and then copy it to your Scripts folder. The path depends on the version you're running, but here it was C:\Program Files\Adobe\Adobe Photoshop CS5 (64 Bit)\Presets\Scripts. You will need to restart Photoshop and then the script should be available under File>Scripts. There are other scripts on the system already besides the ones in that folder. Have a look in the main Photoshop program file for a folder called Scripting rather than Presets. You should find Sample Scripts where there are lots of effects to play around with from the JavaScript collection including comparing and converting colours.

Scripts Event Manager
Automate your workflow

Go to File>Scripts>Script Event Manager. This is the automated event window that can be configured to launch scripts or actions when a specific Photoshop event occurs. The default events are based around file actions like creating new documents, closing, opening and saving documents. You can even have a script run as soon as Photoshop launches. If, for example, you process a lot of digital photographs, you can have the event set as Open Document and the script set to Display Camera Manufacturer. Another useful one is, on saving a file, to automatically save a JPEG version of it at the same time. Tick the Enable Events box and select the event and action you want.

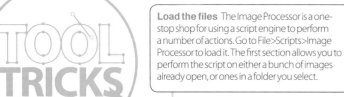

Load the files The Image Processor is a one-stop shop for using a script engine to perform a number of actions. Go to File>Scripts>Image Processor to load it. The first section allows you to perform the script on either a bunch of images already open, or ones in a folder you select.

Save the results Processed files can be saved in the same location. Sub-folders are also supported for both import and export. Don't worry about overwriting files though. Each of the file formats is created in its own named directory so the originals are preserved.

Resize to fit The Image Processor is good for batch resizing as well. In the third section there are also options for converting the current colour profile to sRGB and then resizing for web use.

Choose a file type If the process is going to add layers to the image, it's a good idea to use a file format that supports it, otherwise the results will be flattened. You can save as JPEG, PSD or TIFF, the latter two supporting layers.

Take action There's a selection of actions that you can run on the files as well. The one selected here is a sepia toning layer. The reason for using the Image Processor here is that there are four images and this will give each a sepia toning. You can then look at them all and decide which one is best.

Use shortcuts
Assign keys to your favourite scripts

It you find that there's one particular script that you use all the time it makes sense to assign it a keyboard shortcut so it can be run even more quickly. Go to Edit>Keyboard Shortcuts. Choose Application Menus and scroll down the command list until you get to Scripts and then your favourite one. Click on it and the Shortcut box will appear. Don't try to type the shortcut,

instead, press the key combination you want. If that is already being used you will be warned and given the option to try again or overwrite the existing shortcut. Once accepted click on OK to save.

Find great scripts!
Here's a favourite one at work

There are loads of free scripts available from generous people out there. Try photo sites like Flickr as a starting point. There's a great LOMO camera effect script from Christopher Holland

that makes your photos look like they were taken with the cheap and cheerful Russian LOMO camera from the Eighties. It's entirely automatic but leaves you with the layer structure for elements such as blur, vignetting and over-saturation to play with. Install and run as usual.

Using Save for Web

Need to get your images ready to go online? Shave the size using the Save for Web command

Even with broadband and increasingly nippy web speeds, a hefty image file size is a sure route to frustration. Altering image size is usually tackled using the aptly named Image Size command, but it can sometimes be a juggling act between shrinking the size and keeping quality. A solution lies with the Save for Web command. Found in the File menu, it works in a separate window and gives you the option to have a before and after view so you can clearly see what effect the edit has had on your image.

Top tip: Use the Hand and Zoom tools within the Save for Web window to navigate around your image and check what effect the edit has had on image quality.

PLAY THE SHRINKING GAME
Get svelte images for sharing online

01 Open the dialog Load the image you want to reduce in Photoshop and then go to File>Save for Web. A new window will appear. Head up to the top-left area and click the 2-Up tab. This will give you a before and after view. Now go down to the bottom-right area (where it says 100%) and select Fit on Screen to change this and see everything.

02 Clock the numbers Go over to the Preset area on the far right. Select JPEG (or pick another preferred format from the drop-down menu) and then turn to the menu below this. Here you will find some default settings for reducing file size. Obviously the higher the quality the higher the file size.

03 See the change If you look underneath the before and after areas, you will discover some file sizes (the original and the edited size). Go up to the Quality drop-down menu and select another setting. Let Photoshop do its thing and then look at the size to see if it's suitable. Keep editing until happy and then click Save.

Layer up filters

Expand the functionality of Photoshop filters by applying more than one using the layer option

Filters are a fantastic way of achieving effects that would otherwise take a fair chunk of time to produce manually. Although you can control the filters using sliders, there is also another way of ensuring you get the result you want. And that is by layering the filters. It's easy to miss this feature, but look in the bottom-right of the Filter Gallery and you'll see a little layer icon. This is actually called New effect layer and, once clicked, lets you apply another

Top tip: Your multi-layered filter odyssey only lasts as long as you are in the Filter Gallery. Make sure you carry out any edits you need while in this area.

PREPARE FOR FILTER ONSLAUGHT
Create your own filter layer cake

01 **Set yourself up** Open up your image and go to Filter>Filter Gallery. Pop down to the bottom-left and use the arrow to pick a view option; Fit in Screen works well. Now go to the middle panel and click an arrow to see the filters in that set. Pick one you like and adjust the sliders to get the effect you want.

02 **Add a new filter** Go down to the bottom-right and click the button that looks like a New Layer icon (it is actually called 'New effect layer'). A new layer will appear in the area above. The default is a duplicate of the filter already applied. Simply select another filter to make it appear on the new layer.

03 **More filter management** You can build up more and more filter layers, depending on your needs. It is also possible to turn the visibility of layers off, as well as remove them (use the Delete effect layer icon). Click and drag on a filter layer to alter its position in the stack.

Photoshop shortcuts

Speed up your workflow with these handy shortcuts

Once you've got to grips with the basic Photoshop tools and features, it's a great idea to start practising some of the shortcuts.

Those used to working with Photoshop on a daily basis rely almost entirely on shortcuts to create their work. Over these two pages we've compiled an essential shortcut guide, which we've split into sections based on the type of tasks you perform. Make sure you have this cut-out-and-keep guide close to your computer and use it whenever you have a Photoshop project on the go. We're certain you will know these shortcuts off by heart in no time!

HANDY SHORTCUTS FOR EVERYDAY TOOLS

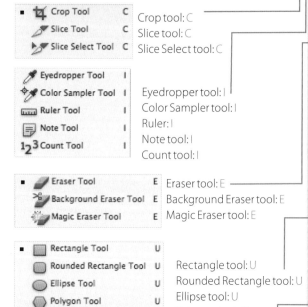

Crop Tool C	Crop tool: C
Slice Tool C	Slice tool: C
Slice Select Tool C	Slice Select tool: C

Eyedropper Tool I	Eyedropper tool: I
Color Sampler Tool I	Color Sampler tool: I
Ruler Tool I	Ruler: I
Note Tool I	Note tool: I
123 Count Tool I	Count tool: I

Eraser Tool E	Eraser tool: E
Background Eraser Tool E	Background Eraser tool: E
Magic Eraser Tool E	Magic Eraser tool: E

Rectangle Tool U	Rectangle tool: U
Rounded Rectangle Tool U	Rounded Rectangle tool: U
Ellipse Tool U	Ellipse tool: U
Polygon Tool U	Polygon tool: U
Line Tool U	Line tool: U
Custom Shape Tool U	Custom Shape tool: U

Hand Tool H	Hand tool: H
Rotate View Tool R	Hand tool: Spacebar

SELECT AND SELECTION TOOLS

Rectangular Marquee Tool M	Rectangular Marquee tool: M
Elliptical Marquee Tool M	Elliptical Marquee tool: M
Single Row Marquee Tool	Single Row Marquee tool: M
Single Column Marquee Tool	Single Column Marquee tool: M

Lasso tool: L
Polygonal Lasso tool: L
Magnetic Lasso tool: L

Lasso Tool L	
Polygonal Lasso Tool L	
Magnetic Lasso Tool L	

Magic Wand tool: W
Quick Selection Tool: W

Quick Selection Tool W	
Magic Wand Tool W	

Toggle Standard/Quick Mask modes: Q
Cycle Path/Direct Selection tools: Shift+A
Toggle Slice/Slice Select tools: Shift+K
Cycle Lasso tools: Shift+L
Toggle Rectangular/Elliptical Marquee: Shift+M
Toggle Pen/Freeform Pen tools: Shift+P
Select All: Cmd/Ctrl+A
Select All Layers: Cmd+Opt+A/Ctrl+Alt+A
Deselect: Cmd/Ctrl+D
Feather: Cmd+Opt+D/Ctrl+Alt+D
Inverse: Cmd/Ctrl+Shift+I
Reselect: Cmd/Ctrl+Shift+D

PAINTING TOOLS

Brush Tool B	Brush tool: B
Pencil Tool B	Pencil tool: B
Color Replacement Tool B	Color Replacement tool: B
Mixer Brush Tool B	Mixer Brush tool: B

Decrease/Increase Brush Size: [/]
Decrease/Increase Brush Hardness: {/}
Previous Brush: ,
Next Brush: .
First Brush: <
Last Brush: >
Brush tool: B
Pencil tool: B
Gradient tool: G
Paint Bucket tool: G
Sponge tool: O

History Brush Tool Y	
Art History Brush Tool Y	

History Brush tool: Y
Art History Brush Tool: B
Tool Opacity 10%-100%: 1-0
Flow/Airbrush Opacity 10%-100%: Shift+ 1-0

Zoom tool: Z

IMAGE-EDITING TOOLS

Spot Healing Brush tool: J
Healing Brush tool: J
Patch tool: J
Red Eye tool: J

- Spot Healing Brush Tool — J
- Healing Brush Tool — J
- Patch Tool — J
- Red Eye Tool — J

Clone Stamp tool: S
Pattern Stamp tool: S

- Clone Stamp Tool — S
- Pattern Stamp Tool — S

Dodge tool: O
Burn tool: O

- Dodge Tool — O
- Burn Tool — O

Toggle Clone/Pattern Stamp: Shift+S
Auto Color: Cmd/Ctrl+Shift+B
Auto Contrast: Cmd+Opt+Shift+I /Ctrl+Alt+Shift+L
Auto Levels: Cmd/Ctrl+Shift+L
Canvas Size: Cmd+Opt+C/Ctrl+Alt+C
Color Balance: Cmd/Ctrl+B
Color Balance (last settings): Cmd+Opt+M/
Ctrl+Alt+M
Curves (last settings): Cmd+Opt+M/Ctrl+Alt+M
Curves: Cmd/Ctrl+M
Desaturate: Cmd/Ctrl+Shift+U
Hue/Saturation: Cmd/Ctrl+U
Hue/Saturation (last settings): Cmd+Opt+U/
Ctrl+Alt+U
Image size: Cmd+Opt+I/Ctrl+Alt+I
Invert: Cmd/Ctrl+I
Levels: Cmd/Ctrl+L
Levels (last settings): Cmd+Opt+L/Ctrl+Alt+L

Foreground/Background colours
Default colours: D
Switch colours: X
Edit in Quick Mask Mode: Q

MORE TOOLS TO PLAY WITH IN PHOTOSHOP

- Gradient Tool — G
- Paint Bucket Tool — G

Gradient tool: G
Paint Bucket tool: G

- Hand Tool — H
- Rotate View Tool — R

Hand tool: H
Rotate View tool: R

TYPE TOOLS

- T Horizontal Type Tool — T
- T Vertical Type Tool — T
- Horizontal Type Mask Tool — T
- Vertical Type Mask Tool — T

Horizontal Type tool: T
Vertical Type tool: T
Horizontal Type Mask tool: T
Vertical Type Mask tool: T

- Path Selection Tool — A
- Direct Selection Tool — A

Path Selection tool: A
Direct Selection tool: A

Align Left: Cmd/Ctrl+Shift+L
Align Right: Cmd/Ctrl+Shift+R
Bold (toggle): Cmd/Ctrl+Shift+B
Centre text: Cmd/Ctrl+Shift+C
Decrease/Increase Type Size by 10pt:
Cmd+Opt+ Shift+<, /Ctrl+Alt+Shift+<, >
Hyphenation (toggle): Cmd+Opt+Shift+H/
Ctrl+Alt+Shift+H
Italics (toggle): Cmd/Ctrl+Shift+I
Justify Paragraph (Force last line): Cmd/Ctrl+Shift+F
Justify Paragraph (Left align last line): Cmd/Ctrl+Shift+J
Underlining (toggle): Cmd/Ctrl+Shift+U
Uppercase (toggle): Cmd/Ctrl+Shift+K

LAYERS

Bring Forward: Cmd/Ctrl+]
Bring to Front: Cmd/Ctrl+Shift+]
Create/Release Clipping Mask (toggle): Cmd+Opt+G/
Ctrl+Alt+G
Group Layers: Cmd/Ctrl+G
Layer Opacity 10%-100%: 1-0
Layer Via Copy: Cmd+ Opt+J/Ctrl+Alt+J
Layer Via Copy (with dialog): Cmd/Ctrl+Shift+I
Merge Layers: Cmd/Ctrl+E Merge Visible: Cmd/Ctrl+Shift+E
New Layer: Cmd/Ctrl+Shift+N
New Layer (no dialog): Cmd+Opt+Shift+N/Ctrl+Alt+Shift+N
Next Layer: Opt/Alt+]
Previous Layer: Opt/Alt+[
Select Previous Layer: Opt/Alt+Shift+[
Select Next Layer: Opt/Alt+Shift+]
Send Backward: Cmd/Ctrl+[
Send to Back: Cmd/Ctrl+Shift+[
Stamp Down: Cmd+Opt+E/Ctrl+Alt+E
Stamp Visible: Cmd+Opt+Shift+E/Ctrl+Alt+Shift+E
Select Bottom Layer: Opt/Alt+, Select Top Layer: Opt/Alt+.

Troublesho

Whatever version of Photoshop you use, we solve your burning issues with answers from the experts

How can you control brushes and make them work for you?

What are styles, and how do you use them?

Top tip: Photoshop forums are great places to go for advice, as you can get instant feedback from the community whatever version of the program you use.

oting

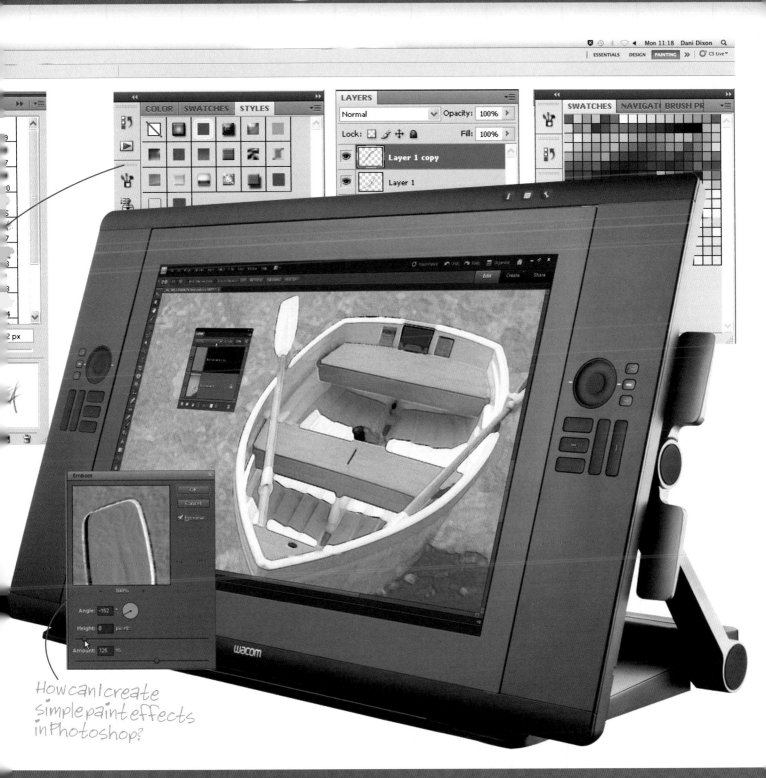

How can I create
simple paint effects
in Photoshop?

Q&A
Photoshop Elements

Perfect panoramas

Q Any tips on shooting images for a Photomerge panorama? The colours and exposure tend to change when I do it.
Andy Baker

A If you shoot on Auto the camera will adjust the aperture and shutter speed settings to try and achieve a balanced exposure. This is fine for a single shot, but when stitching multiple images together you need a consistent exposure or the sky could be lighter in

one shot and darker in the next. This exposure change can produce noticeable joins in your stitched together panorama. Photoshop's Photomerge command can create a gentle blend between each image, but you'll get better results if your source photos have the same exposure values.

When shooting your panorama's source images pop the camera on the Manual setting. You can then choose a relatively narrow aperture like f/8 to help keep foreground and background objects in focus. Set the shutter speed so that enough light is entering the camera 's aperture to

capture a healthy exposure. Set the focal point on a distant object then lock the focus. If the camera changes its focal point while you take the separate shots, they won't stitch together very effectively.

Most people shoot panoramic source images with a handheld camera, which can cause you to tilt up as you pan. The Photomerge command can reposition the images to align them, but will create transparent areas around the edge of the frame. Elements 9's Photomerge command attempts to replace these areas, but you should try to get it right when shooting.

Tips & fixes

Restore sky colour

When shooting a landscape to create a panorama, you may find the sky becomes burnt out when you shoot too near the sun. This can cause an uneven sky that is blue in one area and white in another. To paint the white sky blue, grab the Brush tool. Hold down Opt/Alt and click to sample some original blue sky. The Foreground Color will change to the sampled blue and the brush will paint with that colour. Set the brush's mode to Multiply. Now the white sky will be replaced by blue, leaving other areas of the image unaltered.

"With Photomerge... you'll get better results if your source photos have the same exposure values"

On Manual mode you can capture a consistent exposure for your panorama's source images

Photomerge
Say goodbye to vignetting

If you shoot panoramic source images with the lens fully zoomed out, you run the risk of capturing darker (vignetted) areas at the corners of the frame. These patches will make it more difficult to stitch the shots seamlessly together. The camera's lens can also cause straight lines to become curved at the edges, creating another stitching challenge. Fortunately Elements 9's Photomerge command has new boxes to tick if you need to overcome vignetting and lens distortion.

The revamped Photomerge can overcome lens-related artifacts

RESOURCES: TUTORIAL
We touch on the importance of getting the exposure correct when shooting panoramas here. To delve a
bit deeper into the subject of exposure check out Geoff Lawrence's comprehensive article on the subject.
www.geofflawrence.com/photography_tutorial_exposure.php

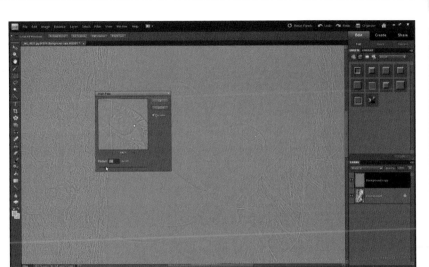

See exactly which areas will be sharpened using the High Pass filter

High pass sharpening

Q I find it difficult to understand how Photoshop's sharpening filter works. Can you explain how to sharpen more easily and effectively?
Natalie Wright

A Occasionally we like to trot out the acronym G.I.G.O – Garbage In, Garbage Out. This certainly applies to sharpening. If a shot isn't sharp to start with, then Photoshop can only do so much to reveal finer details. Elements' Adjust Sharpness command creates a sharper looking shot by increasing the contrast around the edge of objects in the image, making delicate details stand out. However, if you use too large a contrast change then you run the risk of adding dark or light halos to the edge of your subject's features. The Adjust Sharpness command has a Radius slider that lets you increase the spread the of the contrast change. This can also exaggerate these halo artifacts.

The problem with Adjust Sharpness is that you can't clearly see which edges are having their contrast adjusted. If the shot has lots of picture noise due to a high ISO setting, then the sharpening process can also exaggerate these unwanted artifacts. Luckily there is a sharpening technique that works in the same way as Adjust

Sharpness, but it also enables you to see exactly which features will be sharpened. Open a soft focus image like our portrait. Drag the Background layer onto the Create a new layer icon to make a copy. Go to Filter>Other>High Pass. Adjust the Radius slider until only important details (like eyes and hair) are visible, and unimportant areas (like picture noise) aren't. Click OK. Change the greyscale High Pass layer's blending mode to Soft Light. Only the areas that were visible on the High Pass layer will be affected by sharpening.

DAMAGED PHOTO
Encourage signs of aging

Q We see lots of tutorials on fixing damage in old scanned prints, but how can I go about 'distressing' a modern digital shot?
Amber Burke

A Begin the aging quest by finding a suitable source photo with a retro style subject. To create organic looking damage, download an image featuring an abstract texture. We also use Elements 9 as this gave us easy access to layer masks.

01 **Add mask** Double-click the Background image. Click the 'Add layer mask' icon. Open your texture. Select>All and Copy. Opt/Alt-click the mask and paste the texture into it.

02 **Add dirt** Create a new layer. Choose Edit>Fill layer. Use 50% Gray. Drag this layer below the Background layer. Organic bits of grey will appear over your main photo like smudges of dirt.

03 **Tint it** Choose Layer>New Adjustment Layer>Hue/Saturation. Tick Colorize to turn the shot into monotone. Drag Hue to around 31 to add a retro wash of sepia.

Photoshop Elements

Photomerge action shots

Q How can I go about shooting lots of images of a fast-moving subject (like someone diving into water), and then merging several shots into a single image that shows the subject's movement?

Nathan Wright

A A composite image is a great way to portray movement, especially after photographing sporty subjects like a jumping horse. The trick to making a successful composite action shot is to shoot a series of stills. To do this, use a digital SLR that has a continuous shooting (or burst) mode. This enables you to capture multiple versions of the subject as the action unfolds. Set the camera to Shutter Priority (S) mode so that you can force it to shoot with a fast shutter speed (like 1/320 sec). This helps reduce motion blur on fast-moving objects like our horse. Try and shoot the action from side-on or you may find that the moving subject will overlap itself as it travels across the frame, making it tricky to separate the various versions of the subject in the edited composite image.

We shot four images of a horse jumping a fence. To mix shots like these together open them in Elements. Go to File>New>Photomerge Group Shot. Choose Open All. If the photos were taken handheld, then Photomerge will automatically align them. Drag the best shot into the Final box on the right. Then select the Pencil tool and click on the other images one by one in the Project bin. Scribble over the horse in each source image and it will be automatically added to the composite image in the Final window. Click Done when you're happy with the finished result.

Photomerge can help you to create a complex composite

Tips & fixes

Use a tripod

When compositing multiple shots together (see the first question), Photomerge normally does a good job of auto-aligning the source files so that the background details will merge perfectly in the final image. However Photomerge does demand a lot of RAM, especially when dealing with large source images. This can cause the package to hang on machines that don't have enough memory. If you shoot your source files on a tripod then they will already be aligned, giving Photoshop less work to do. You'll also avoid the need to crop out transparent edges caused by Photomerge's auto-alignment process.

> "A composite image is a great way to portray movement, especially with sporty subjects"

Evoke action by merging consecutive shots into a composite image

RESOURCES: INSPIRATION

If you need more inspiration for suitable subjects to use in an action sequence composite, check out Kaan Kiran's walkthrough at DIY Photography's site. It gives insights into shooting source photos for this kind of creative kinetic project.
www.diyphotography.net/composing-an-action-sequence-shot

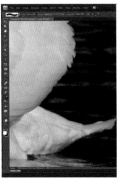
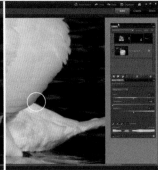

Paint away unsightly colour fringes using adjustment layers

Colour fringing

Q I notice in some walkthroughs that people use Photoshop's Lens Correction filter to remove chromatic aberration. The Elements version of that filter doesn't have these tools. How do we remove colour fringes?
Chris Wyatt

A Chromatic aberration refers to the fringes of colour that cling to the edge of high contrast objects. Our white swan has noticeable cyan and magenta fringes around its outline, for example. These fringes tend to be worse on images captured by a camera with a small sensor, although a camera with a larger megapixel rating and a professional L-series lens can still produce colour fringes.

Although Elements lacks a dedicated chromatic aberration correction command, there is an effective workaround. Open a problem image (like our swan shot) and zoom in to 100% to see the fringes more clearly. Open the Layers palette and click the Create New Fill or Adjustment Layer icon. Choose a Hue/Saturation adjustment layer. Click the Master drop-down menu and choose Cyan. Drag the Saturation slider to –100 and the cyan fringe will vanish. Set the drop-down menu to Magenta and reduce Saturation to 100. If you have any other fringe colours you can target and desaturate those too.

"Although Elements lacks a dedicated chromatic aberration correction tool, there is a workaround"

It's likely there will be some magenta or cyan in other parts of the shot that you need to preserve. Click on the Hue/Saturation adjustment layer's white mask and press Cmd/Ctrl+I to invert it. The white mask will turn black, protecting the colours in the image from being adjusted. You can now paint a white brush on the black mask to selectively desaturate the colour fringes.

Desaturate
Final fixing

We demonstrate how to target and desaturate specific colour fringes in the above question. If that technique leaves behind traces of other colours (like green for example), grab the Sponge tool from the Tools palette. In the Options bar, set the Sponge tool's Mode to Desaturate. Set Flow to 100%. You can now spray a small soft round brush tip over any remaining colour fringes to mop them up. Use the square bracket keys on your keyboard to quickly shrink or enlarge the brush tip as you work.

Quickly remove stray colour fringes by desaturating them

AUTO COLOR
Liven up skin tones

Q I've taken a shot with the wrong colour balance setting, so it's very blue. Auto Color Correction warms it up a bit, but the skin tones still look a little cold. Do you have any tips?
Gareth Simpson

A In Photoshop CS you can use Color Balance. However, this command is lacking in Elements. The Color Variations command enables you to counteract tints by adding warmer colours.

01 **Auto Color** Go to Enhance>Auto Color Correction. This should warm things up and banish most of the blues. However the shot may still look cold. We can fine-tune with Auto Adjustment.

02 **Variations** Go to Enhance>Adjust Color>Color Variations and tick Midtones. Reduce the Amount slider. Click the Increase Red thumbnail to warm up the midtones. Click Decrease Blue to take away the chilly tint.

03 **Fine-tune** Click the Shadows button and increase the Red with a couple of clicks. Color Variations let you target specific tones. Remove the green tint on the skin tones with a click or two on Decrease Green.

Photoshop Elements

Exposure compensation

Q When I shoot snow it tends to look grey instead of white. Why is this and how can I fix the problem in Photoshop Elements?

Jenny Knight

A Most digital cameras tend to use matrix metering when setting an exposure. This means that they take a light reading of the whole scene, then they average the amount of light entering the camera to try and get a balanced exposure. When faced with the glare of light bouncing off a snowy landscape, your camera will tend to under-expose the scene in an attempt to capture highlight detail. This can make snow look grey, rather than white. Many digital SLRs have an exposure compensation command that enables you to open up the aperture electronically to let in more light, and make snow (or any bright white source, like a wedding dress) look white.

To fake exposure compensation in Photoshop, duplicate the image by dragging its thumbnail onto the Create New Layer icon at the bottom of the Layers palette, then grab the Dodge tool. Choose a large soft brush tip from the Brush Preset picker. In the Options bar set Range to Highlights. This stops the brush brightening the photo's correctly exposed shadows and midtones. Set Exposure to a low value

"Set up your Dodge tool and spray it over the under-exposed grey snow to turn it white"

Brighten up under-exposed snow with the Dodge tool in Photoshop

Tips & fixes

Save with layers

By using an adjustment layer to change a JPEG's colours, you can alter its effect at any time to fine-tune your image. Simply double-click on the adjustment layer's thumbnail to see its editable attributes. However, when you save the file, make sure that you preserve the adjustment layer so that you can tweak it at a later date. If you save the file as a flattened JPEG, the adjustment layer will vanish. Go to File>Save As. Set the Format drop-down menu to one that supports layers, like TIFF or PSD for example.

Change the opacity
Use layers to preserve detail

In the above question we used the Dodge tool to brighten up dull snow. If you end up over-exposing the snow you can use Cmd/Ctrl+Z to undo the last few strokes. However, if you close the file then your edit history is lost. By dodging the snow on a duplicate layer you can restore detail to blown-out highlights by reducing the opacity on the edited layer. This reveals some of the original snow on the layer below maintaining a balance between increasing brightness and preserving detail.

Reduce the intensity of an edit but keep detail by adjusting layer opacity

like 5% as this will enable the Dodge tool to lighten the highlights in gentle increments and avoid blowing them out quickly and losing too much detail.

Once you've set up your Dodge tool, simply spray it over the under-exposed grey snow to turn it white. Other tones (like the soldier in our example image) should remain relatively untouched.

Selective colour adjustments

 What's the quickest and easiest way to turn most of an image black and white but preserve the colours in specific objects?

Tim Morgan

 By preserving the colour of a specific object you can make it stand out from a predominantly black-and-white scene.

However, some objects can be tricky to select in the first place. The red berries in our start image are scattered throughout the shot and are covered in snow, making it a challenge to make a selection around them using traditional techniques like the Magic Wand tool. You could try desaturating the shot's blue background while preserving the berries' colour by going to Enhance>Adjust Color>Replace Color. By clicking the Eyedropper tool on the blue sky you should be able to select all of the sky, then reduce its Saturation to −100. This will turn the sky to monochrome while leaving the red berry colour untouched, but it can be a long-winded process, fine-tuning with the Add to Sample eyedropper and adjusting the Fuzziness slider.

For faster colour control, go to the Layers palette and click the Create New Adjustment Layer icon. Add a Hue/Saturation adjustment layer. Click on the Master drop-down menu and choose Blues. Drop Saturation to −100 and desaturate the cyans too in case there are traces of that colour in the sky. Target and desaturate other colours like the yellow tree branch, leaving the red berries untouched.

To enhance the berries' colour even more, set the drop-down menu to Reds and pop the Saturation slider up to around +56. This technique gives you a faster and cleaner way to target and adjust specific colours than you'd get if you were trying to make changes with a standard selection tool.

> ## "This technique gives you a fast and clean way to target and adjust specific colours"

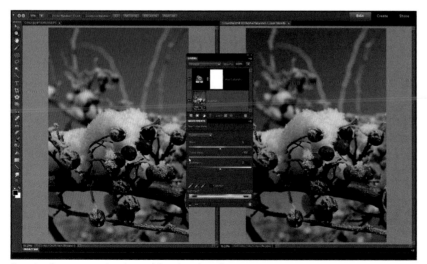

Target and remove certain colours while enhancing others

FUR EFFECT
Create hair-raising text

 I've been on a mission to make fluffy text for a friend's website – all furry and soft-looking like the funny dice people have in their cars. Any help you could give me would be great.
The Perdactor

 Photoshop Elements lacks the power of paths that you would use for this in Photoshop CS, so here's an alternative way to make fur grow out from text for users of this version.

01 **Create text** Grab the Horizontal Type tool and type out some text. Use a soft curvy font. Cmd/Ctrl-click on the text layer's thumbnail to select it then hide the layer using the eye icon.

02 **Brush tip** Choose the Dune Grass brush. Choose different shades of brown for the Foreground and Background Colors and create a new layer. Paint into the text-shaped selection marquee.

03 **Spray fur** Choose Select>Inverse. Now spray fur sprouting from the edge of the letters. To make the fur grow in different directions, click the Brush Dynamics icon and change the Angle.

Photoshop Elements

Tackle high contrast

 I have a portrait that was taken in bright sunlight so the skin is overexposed and the shadows lack detail. How can I restore this in the contrasting tones?

John Bridgman

 Strong sunlight gives your camera's metering mode a challenge due to the extreme difference in exposure between the sunlit highlights and the darkest shadows. The metering mode can decide to set the aperture and shutter speed to reveal shadow details, but this will cause areas in direct sunlight to become overexposed and lack detail (like our subject's sunlit skin in the example image). Alternatively, the camera may capture the texture on sunlit skin, but dramatically darken the subject's shaded eyes and hair to lose all detail.

The Levels command works well when lightening or darkening midtones, but it can't claw back missing detail in overexposed highlights or reveal detail in very clipped shadows. Luckily Photoshop Elements has another command up its sleeve to help you lighten shadows, reveal blown-out highlight details and improve your picture.

Go to Enhance>Adjust Lighting> Shadows>Highlights. This command is designed to recover detail in backlit shots, so the Lighten Shadows slider is automatically set to 25%. This default amount is enough to reveal our subject's eyes in this example, but their sunlit skin is still overexposed. To claw back detail, slide Darken Highlights to around 19%. You can also tweak midtone contrast if required then click OK.

Target and reveal detail in shadows and highlights

Tips & fixes

Check your layer's edit
Before you start adjusting your portrait's shadows and highlights as in the above question (or any high contrast shot), open the Layers palette (Window>Layers) and drag the locked Background layer onto the Create a New Layer icon to create an editable duplicate. Once you've edited the duplicate's shadows and highlights you can click the top layer's eye icon to toggle between a before and after version of the image. You can also reduce the top layer's opacity to mix the edited image's tones with some of the original's shadows and highlights to fine-tune the final look of the picture.

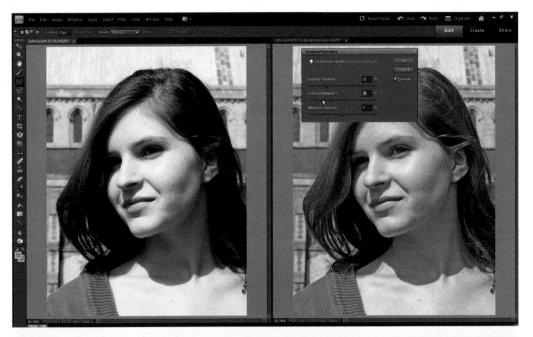

Metering modes
Capture specific tonal detail

Photoshop can reveal hidden shadow detail, but this can cause the edited shadows to display compression artifacts and look desaturated. By default most cameras try and average the light in a scene to compromise between shadows and highlights. They do this using a Matrix metering mode that takes a light reading from multiple points in the viewfinder. By setting the metering mode to Spot (or Partial) you can press the shutter button halfway to take the light reading of a more specific area. This helps you prioritise which areas need to show detail.

Metering mode

Spot metering

Prioritise the important tones when shooting

RESOURCES: TUTORIALS

To learn more about the techniques and science behind in-camera light metering, check out this site. It could give you insight into how your camera tackles various conditions.
www.cambridgeincolour.com/tutorials/camera-metering.htm

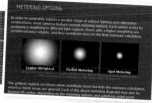

As a finishing touch you can apply a Levels adjustment layer to make sure that the shot still has some black shadows and white highlights. This ensures that the image retains contrast and doesn't look flat.

Tilt-shift effect

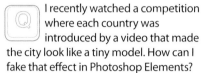

Q I recently watched a competition where each country was introduced by a video that made the city look like a tiny model. How can I fake that effect in Photoshop Elements?
Colette Tanner

A When you shoot a real model like a train set, you're much closer to the subject than you would be to a full-size scene. This proximity causes the camera to shoot with a very shallow depth of field, making foreground and background details look out of focus. Only a narrow band of detail remains sharp on the most foreground elements.

When shooting a city, you could pop a specialist tilt-shift lens onto the camera to creatively adjust the scene's focal point and mimic this shallow depth of field. However, tilt-shift lenses are expensive and fiddly to use, so it makes more sense to re-create the effect using layers and filters – and luckily it is easy to do.

To turn a city into a toy town, take the shot from a high vantage point (as if you were looming over your model). Open it in Elements and drag the locked Background layer onto the Create a new layer icon to duplicate it. Target the Background copy layer by clicking on its thumbnail and go to Filter>Blur>Gaussian Blur. Use a Radius of 9 and click OK. Click the Add layer mask icon with the blurred layer selected.

Grab the Gradient tool and set it to the Foreground to Background preset. Click the Reflected Gradient icon in the Options bar and tick the Reverse icon. Press 'D' to set Foreground and Background Colors to the default black and white. Click and drag on the layer mask to draw a narrow black band surrounded by white. The darker areas will make the blur disappear, revealing a narrow band of sharp details on the layer below, giving the tilt-shift effect.

> "To turn a city into a toy town, take the shot from a high vantage point, as if you were looming over your model"

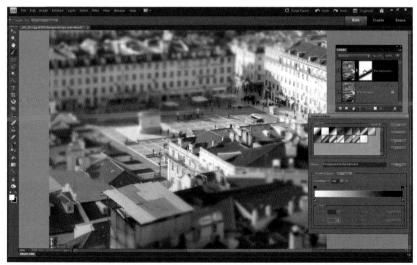

Mimic a specialist lens and make a vast city look like a toy town

THICK STROKES
Mimic an oil painting

Q How can I make a filtered photo look like it consists of thick, raised brushstrokes – like an oil painting?
Thomas Fullum

A It's easy enough to slap an artistic filter onto a shot to make it look more like a painting, but the shot will lack the thick strokes produced by blobs of paint. We have a cool technique that gives your strokes a convincing 3D edge; just follow these simple steps.

01 Apply filter Open a photo then go to Filter>Artistic>Paint Daubs. Set Brush Size to 23 and Sharpness to 4. Set Brush Type to Dark Rough to create the brushstrokes and click OK to apply.

02 Duplicate layer Duplicate the filtered layer. Go to Filter> Stylize>Emboss and set the Angle to -152 degrees, Height to 8 and Amount to 125%. This adds thick raised lines. Click OK.

03 Change blend Go to Enhance> Adjust Color> Remove Color, then set its blending mode to Overlay. This removes the grey but preserves the thick lines.

Photoshop CS and above

WATER DROP MAGNIFICATION

Q I really want to create a water drop on top of some text but I really don't know where to begin. Can you help?

Nicholas Faulkner

A Water drops are pretty easy to make using the Dodge and Burn tools. The Dodge tool makes pixels lighter while the Burn tool makes them darker. We will also need to make use of the Spherize filter.

01 **Background and text** Make a new document and fill the background with a light colour. Use the Text tool and a fairly bold font to write something.

02 **Drawing the drop** Create a new layer above the text layer, select the Elliptical Marquee tool and draw out an oval over the top of part of the text. Next select Edit>Copy Merged followed by Edit>Paste.

03 **Dodge and Burn** Select the oval by Cmd/Ctrl-clicking its thumbnail in the Layers palette. Go to Filter>Distort> Spherize. Emphasise the shape using the Dodge and Burn tools.

Clone Stamp tool vs Healing Brush tool

Q I'm interested in finding out what is better – the Clone Stamp or the Healing tools for removing objects from pictures?

Taylor Nelson

A This is an interesting question, because although they all do a similar job they do things very differently. The Clone tool will copy different parts of a picture or layer after a source has been specified by holding the Opt/Alt key on your keyboard. Just like using a normal brush, the shape, opacity, spacing and hardness (to name a few) can all be specified using the Brush palette. As for the Healing tools, you have two to choose from: the Healing Brush tool and the Spot Healing Brush tool. The Healing Brush tool works similarly to the Clone Stamp in that you specify an area to sample and Photoshop tries to intelligently blend the sampled area and the area you wish to heal together. Unlike the Clone Stamp, you cannot set the brush style, but you can edit the size, hardness and spacing. The tool also allows you to edit the angle and roundness, so you can change the shape slightly. For example, dropping the roundness to 50% will give you a oval shape. The Spot Healing Brush works similarly but you do

> ## "The Clone tool will copy different parts of a picture after a source has been specified"

It's possible to use the Healing Brush tool just like any other brush

not specify the source. The types of healing available are Proximity Match, Create Texture and new to CS5, Content-Aware.

Photo to sketch

Q I want to make a digital photo look like a pencil drawing, I have no artistic talent at all but I've been told I can do it easily with Photoshop.

Christopher Bates

Healing tools
What are they?

The Healing tools are used to remove elements of a picture we no longer want, be this marks on a photo, such as rips or water marks, or actual things in the photo, for example acne on someone's face. The two different Healing tools allow us to fix these problems simply and quickly. They need you to specify a source to sample and then the tool will try to blend the source and layer together. The Spot Healing tool does not need a source specified, although you can select one if you wish.

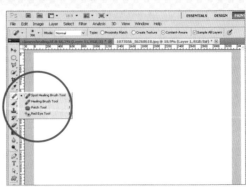

Photoshop's Healing tools allow you to make light work of removing unwanted areas of an image

RESOURCES: BRUSHES

One of the most versatile things about Photoshop is the huge variety of brushes that are available for you to freely use. Brusheezy is a website for artists to download Photoshop brushes, patterns, textures, actions and shapes.
www.brusheezy.com

Using Photoshop we can easily change a photo into a sketch

Smooth gradients can be made using Photoshop's Gradient tool

 There are a number of commercially available filters that will turn a photo into a fairly convincing sketch. Akvis has a sketch program that can either work independently or with Photoshop / Photoshop Elements. This can be purchased from the website at **http://akvis.com/en/sketch/index.php**

We can also use Photoshop to produce a similar effect by utilising an adjustment and a filter. We start by loading a photo into Photoshop and duplicating it, this is to preserve the original just in case we change our minds later. We can duplicate the layer in a couple of different ways – either by dragging the layer to the New Layer icon in the Layers palette or by pressing Cmd/Ctrl+J

on the keyboard. Next we want to remove the colour from the duplicate layer. Once again we can do this in a couple of different ways – the easiest is to just desaturate the layer by going to Image>Adjustments>Desaturate. But we can also use the Black and White adjustment or the Hue/Saturation adjustment. Finally, we run the Find Edges filter from the Filter menu (Filter>Stylize>Find Edges).

Growing gradients

 Can you tell me what gradients are? I've read about them on websites and in your magazine but I'm confused.
Imogen Tomlinson

 When we talk about gradients we are thinking of a smooth transition between two or more colours, for example a blue sky would not be 100% the same colour but would be lighter near the sun and darken when moving away from it. When we use the Gradient tool in Photoshop to produce the same effect, we set the Foreground Color to light blue and the Background Color to dark blue. Then we use the mouse to pull out a gradient across the canvas, in this case from the top to bottom of the canvas. A good tip to keep the gradients straight is to hold the Shift key while you draw out the gradient. This forces the guide to be a straight line and consequently makes the gradient nice and straight.

Healing tools
When is it best to use each tool?

When we want to heal something we can either let Photoshop take control or we can do it ourselves. The key to remember here is that although Photoshop is amazingly clever, it still doesn't have the human element. It can do its best to 'guess' what you

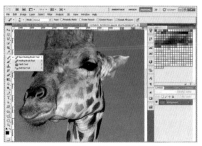

Healing spots and blemishes with the Spot Healing Brush tool

may want but it does not always get it right. As such, using the Spot Healing tool is good way to start, but if it is not giving you the results you want switch to the classic Healing Brush.

Spot Healing options
What are they and how do I use them?

Two different healing types can be found in the Spot Healing Brush options: Proximity Match and Content-Aware. Proximity Match was introduced in CS2 and randomly selects a local area to sample. This is very good for little fixes such as acne. Content-

Content-Aware will try and find areas of continuing colour

Aware Healing is Adobe's new intelligent healing and was introduced in CS5. This tool attempts to blend the sampled area with and area you wish to heal. This option works well things like graffiti.

Photoshop CS and above

EASY MODERN ART
Use filters for striking effect

 Q I want to make a modern art style picture for a friend to use on her website, I've played with the filters but I'm not getting anywhere. Can you help?
Sean Marshall

 A You can create an abstract piece of art by using a couple of filters and adjustments. We have chosen a photo that we will manipulate to create the effect.

01 Posterize the image Duplicate the Background layer and name it 'Cutout'. Next, navigate your way to Image>Adjustments> Posterize, set the number of Levels to 4.

02 The Cutout filter The Cutout filter will reduce the picture to a series of simple shapes. Go to Filter>Artistic> Cutout, set the Number of Levels to 8, the Edge Simplicity to 9 and Edge Fidelity to 1.

03 Glowing Duplicate the Background layer and move it above the Cutout layer. Go to Filter>Stylize>Glowing Edges (Edge Width = 2, Edge Brightness = 20, Smoothness = 5. Set the layer to Screen.

Swapping backgrounds

Q I have a question. I have a photo of a friend that I have removed from the background using the Lasso tool, but I'm not sure how to put this on a new background.
Rebecca Duncan

A One of the most fun things we can do with Photoshop is to transport people to different places and situations by moving them from one scene to another. You have said that you used the Lasso tool to remove your friend, but there are a number of ways we can actually do this. The most precise cut out would be made using the Pen tool to make a selection, but a lot of people find this hard to get used to. Another tool that was introduced in CS3 is the Quick Selection tool that uses a brush to paint around areas that you want to select. This can yield very good results and is often useful when picking up large items.

Once we have our selection made it is a simple case of copying and pasting, but first make sure you are on the correct layer of your source picture – this will probably be the Background layer. Then go to Edit>Copy (or Copy Merged if you want to copy from more than one layer). Finally go to your new document and select Edit>Paste to transport your friend to her new location.

"One of the most fun things we can do is to transport people to different places"

We can use Photoshop to move people or objects to different locations

Zoom query

 Q I often need to zoom in and out of pictures while working on them, is there an easier way than to keep selecting the Magnify tool?
Bradley Burge

A Photoshop's Magnify tool is pretty cool and allows you to zoom in or out of a picture by selecting the appropriate button in the Options bar. The

Clipping masks
What they are and how to use them

Clipping masks are one of those love it or hate it things that people often get very confused about. A clipping mask should not be confused with a layer mask, which is used to show or hide parts of a layer. Instead, we use a clipping mask to contain elements of one layer within specific boundaries of another. For example, if we 'clipped' a layer that contained an image of trees to a layer with a leaf shape, the leaf shape would remain intact but would be filled with the image of the trees.

Clipping masks are useful when filling one layer with the contents of another

RESOURCES: TUTORIALS

Photoshop Lady contains links to the best Photoshop tutorials available from around the world, covering subjects such as textures and patterns as well as 3D, abstract, drawing, text and photo effects.
www.photoshoplady.com

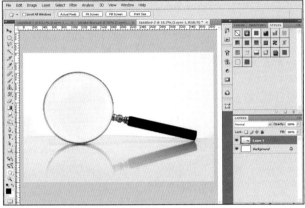

The Magnify tool can be accessed using keyboard shortcuts

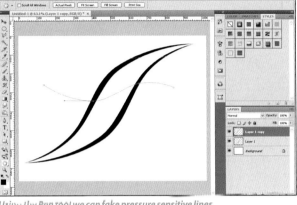

Using the Pen tool we can fake pressure sensitive lines

options available for the Magnify tool are straightforward. The first are Zoom In and Zoom Out, these will increase or decrease the magnification of the current picture. The next option is Zoom All Windows which will keep the same zoom level through multiple open images. The next option, Actual Pixels, will increase the magnification to a ratio of 1:1 so it is at a 100%.

We then have Fit Screen which will change the magnification so it fits the current window size. The Fill Screen option works similarly to the Fit Screen one but will zoom the current window to fit the screen size. Finally we have the Print Size option that will zoom the current window to match the print resolution.

We can also utilise keyboard shortcuts to assist us, holding Cmd/Ctrl and Space will temporarily change the mouse into the Zoom In tool, while holding Opt/Alt and Space will change it to the Zoom Out tool.

Faking pressure sensitivity

 I have noticed line art often tapers out, I assume you do this using a tablet. Is there any way of repeating this effect with a normal mouse?
Jonathan McDonald

 What you're referring to is a phenomenon called pressure sensitivity. This is where you increase

or decrease the pressure on your tablet's stylus to make thicker or thinner lines. This is very useful when drawing, retouching, painting etc, as it gives a realistic effect.

If we wanted to make a tapered line across our canvas, we first start by selecting a Brush from the Brush Library. Any brush can be used but it may be best to start off with a simple Hard Edged one set to around 20 pixels. Next select the Pen tool and make sure Paths are selected in the Options bar. Clicking in two separate locations will make a path, then right-click on the line and select Stroke. Choose the Brush tool from the list of options and tick Simulate Pressure. Finally click OK to draw your line. Try this technique on a drawing for the best results.

Layer masks
Masking is easy and powerful

There is a common misconception that layer masks are not only hard to use but difficult to understand. In reality they are easy to use and they are also extremely powerful. Layer masks are used essentially to hide selected areas of a chosen layer. We

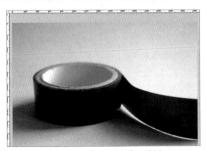

Layer masks are used essentially to hide selected areas of a chosen layer

do this by simply painting on the layer mask with a black brush. We can then unmask an area by using a white brush. We can also vary the opacity of the brush so that the mask is not absolute.

Adjustment layers
Add non-destructive adjustments

Photoshop offers a number of adjustments located in the Image>Adjustment sub-menu. These affect the active layer but will not adjust subsequent layers. The downside to these is that the changes are permanent and can only be edited by going to the History. Adjustment layers offer non-destructive adjustments that can be used over multiple layers or clipped to a single layer. Non-destructive means that you can edit the adjustments at any time without using the history.

Photoshop's adjustment layers offer the capability of non-destructive image editing

Photoshop CS and above

BABY BEARD
Brush on hair for fun effects

 Q Hi, I want to add some facial hair to my son as a joke, but I'm finding it hard to draw it in. Is there any simple way of doing this in Photoshop?
Adam McLean

 A The best way for us to do this is with the Brush tool. It's much easier to alter an existing brush than draw hair freehand. We'll use the Dune Grass brush.

01 **Dune Grass brush** We first select the Brush tool (B) and follow this by pressing F5. In the Brush Presets window (the first tab) locate the Dune Grass brush and click to select it.

02 **Brush Tip Shape** In the second tab down you will see the Brush Tip Shape window. Adjust the angle to -150 degrees. Press F5 on your keyboard again to close the window.

03 **Draw in the hair** On a new layer we brush in some hair around the face, starting on the upper lip and working downwards. Finish with a blur to soften the effect. We chose a Gaussian Blur at 1 pixel.

Photoshop problems

 Q I have a major problem with Photoshop, almost every time I use the program it will crash on me. Could you offer any help?
Dylan Walker

 A There are a number of reasons why programs crash; it could be anything from hardware to software faults. We'll start with the obvious as there is in fact a glitch with Photoshop and occasionally problems arise with the tools. We can fix this by resetting each tool individually or all at once. As you didn't say what tool you were using when it failed lets concentrate on resetting all the tools. Resetting all the tools back to their original state can often fix problems and we do this by first selecting a tool from the Toolbar (it doesn't matter which one). On the Options bar you will see an icon that is the same as the tool you chose, and next to it will be a small down arrow. If you click this arrow you get a window with a number of presets available to you. We want to locate the small arrow on the right of this window. Clicking here will open a menu, then scroll down until you find Reset All Tools and click it.

There are other solutions to this problem however, so check out the boxout below for more ways of fixing Photoshop.

> ## "There are a number of reasons why programs crash; it could be hardware or software faults"

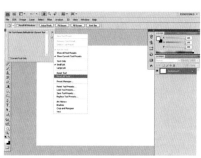

Resetting the tools is one option to help fix problems in Photoshop

HDR in CS5

Q I've been looking at HDR photos and love them. Can I make them in Photoshop?
Katherine Rice

A HDR photography, also known as High Dynamic Range, is a technique that produces photos that look more like their real environment while at the same time giving the scene a

Resetting preferences
Fixing problems before Photoshop loads

Photoshop is a fantastic program that can be used for many different creative projects, but as with most things it occasionally goes wrong. This can be for lots of different reasons and there are lots of solutions (such as the question above). One common cause of headaches is that the Photoshop preferences have become messed up. Luckily for us there is a simple way of resetting these. Simply hold Shift+Cmd/Ctrl+Opt/Alt while Photoshop loads up.

Resetting Photoshop's preferences will cure some of those niggling problems in the program

Use Photoshop's Merge to HDR dialog to produce stunning HDR photos

Photoshop has many available file formats to make life easier

dramatic feel. We can make HDR images by taking multiple photos of the same scene with different exposure values then merging them altogether in one picture.

First, it is essential that you have a camera that has bracketing available. This will take a series of photos using a different exposure for each one, ranging from dark to light. You must have a tripod or a flat surface to balance your camera on so that it does not move.

After we have our series of photos (we need between three and seven for the HDR effect) we can use Photoshop's Merge to HDR Pro in CS5 (or Merge to HDR in CS4 and above) dialog by going to File>Automate>Merge to HDR Pro. Within this dialog box we can edit the merged

photo and create a stunning HDR picture. A full tutorial on how to use Merge to HDR Pro can be found at Tip Squirrel: **http://tinyurl.com/merge2hdr.**

File format

 When I save my pictures in Photoshop I normally use the PSD format, but I noticed there are lots of others available. Which is the best to use?
Charles McGrath

 It all depends on what you want the file for. For example, a PSD file is basically a Photoshop document and can be used with other versions of

Photoshop (as long as the file is compatible with the version you want to open it in). This format will keep the layers intact and is also a file type that is known as lossless – in other words no data is compressed or lost. Another format is a TIFF (Tagged Image File Format). These are normally very large but can be used similarly to a PSD where layers are supported, though they are not recommended for use on the internet.

Other formats that you may be familiar with are JPEG (Joint Photographic Experts Group), PNG (Portable Network Graphics) and GIF (Graphics Interchange Format). These are usually smaller, lossy files, but can be useful in some circumstances, for example with images for websites.

Colored Pencil
Evoke real media easily

The Artistic filters can be used to produce real media effects on photos. The Colored Pencil filter can be found by going to Filter>Artistic Filters>Colored Pencil. When used, it creates a copy of the layer it is on and fills it with a rough, crosshatched

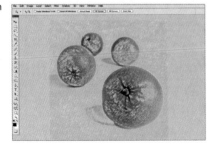

Real media effects can be achieved by using Photoshop's Artistic filters

appearance. Change the colour of the paper it appears on by changing the Background colour. The filter also allows you to edit the pencil width, stroke pressure and paper brightness.

Fibers filter
Create fabric with this Render filter

The Render filters are designed to produce realistic effects and this particular filter creates a texture that is similar to a woven fibre. By setting the colours in the Foreground and Background swatches, you can influence the appearance of the effect. You can also adjust the variance and strength. The Variance slider controls the length of the fibres – a low setting makes long streaks and high creates shorter ones – while the Strength slider controls how each fibre looks.

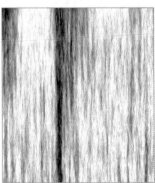

The Fibers filter easily creates a custom woven effect

Photoshop CS and above

CROP TO SIZE
Put your subject centre stage

 Q I want to print out some of my photos and at the moment I'm creating new documents in the size I want, importing the photos to this and then resizing. Is there a better way of doing the same thing?
Angelica Christie

 A The Crop tool has an option to set the crop size either to default options or custom dimensions to suit your needs.

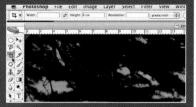

01 **Open the image** Load the photo you want to print in Photoshop. It is a good idea to duplicate the photo so you know you have the original safe somewhere. Go along to the toolbar and select the Crop tool.

02 **Set your boundaries** Go to the top Options bar and look at the Width and Height boxes. These allow you to put in the measurements. Also, make sure that the resolution is the same as your image's.

03 **Crop to fit** Click and drag the Crop tool anywhere in your document. Keep dragging until the crop area fixes at the size you entered. Click and drag over the part you want to print and then double-click.

Create extra canvas

 Q I've started to play around with adding frames to my images and I'm wondering if there is a clever way of doing this? At the moment I am using the Canvas Size command and sometimes have trouble working out the amounts I want.
John Desmond

A The Canvas Size command (found under the Image menu) is the obvious place to go when you need to add more canvas, but as you point out, it can be difficult to visualise how the extra bit you're adding will look. There is a better way, courtesy of the Crop tool. Open up your image and set the background colour to what the extra canvas needs to be.

Click-drag from the bottom-right corner of your document window to expand it – you need to see some grey around your image. Pick the Crop tool and drag out a border for your image. It doesn't matter what size this is. Now use the corner handles of the crop selection and pull these out into the grey area. Anything in the grey will become the extra canvas, so you can see exactly what it will look like. Press Enter on your keyboard to flood the area with your background colour.

Reduce red tone in skin

Q I have lots of holiday photos that I'd like to print but my family all caught the sun rather badly! What's the best way of sorting this out and reducing the redness?
Simon Hastings

The Crop tool can also be used to add extra canvas to your document

Create funky backgrounds
Use the Extrude filter for creative effects

With more and more of us creating scrapbooks or designing pages for photobooks, it's useful to be able to generate background patterns quickly and easily. A good way of doing this is with the Extrude filter. Found under Filter>Stylize, it has a choice of blocks or pyramids. You get to decide how large and deep these are and once you click OK your image will have blocks or pyramids protruding out of it. Try it out on gradient-filled documents or even on photos.

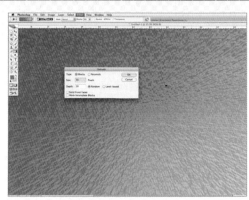

Let the Extrude filter loose and enjoy interesting results

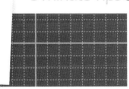

RESOURCES: PHOTOS

Having a good source of stock photos at hand is essential, and morgueFile is an essential stop for image-hungry creatives. There is a staggering range and they're completely free to download.
www.morguefile.com

Quickly calm down red skin with Hue/Saturation

A This is a common problem in holiday photos but it can easily be fixed with the Hue/Saturation command. This command is so good because it provides a way for you to get to the red tones without damaging the overall contrast. The first task is to select the area you want to target. Using your selection tool of choice, pick out the red areas. Because we are making a colour change it's an idea to soften the selection edges to avoid harsh lines. Go to Select>Feather and set a Radius of around 3. Go to Image>Adjustments>Hue/Saturation and pick Reds from the Edit drop-down menu. Drag the Saturation slider to the left. Make sure the Preview box is checked so you can see the change, but uncheck it if you want to see the start image. When you're happy with the changes, just click OK. Press Cmd/Ctrl+D to deselect.

Stamp your copyright

Q I want to set up a website to show my digital paintings and would like a way of adding a copyright to the image previews. Can you give me a quick way of doing this?
Barbara Close

A The easiest way is to make a copyright brush. Create a new document, say 5 x 3 inches with white as the background. Select the Type tool and the font of your choice to write your copyright message (you can use the Opt/Alt key and 'G' to get the copyright symbol). Pick the Rectangular Marquee tool and draw around your text (if you have used different layers make sure to flatten) then go to Edit>Define Brush Preset. Give it a name and stamp it on your image. Now it's saved as a brush you can use it again and again.

Quickly make your mark using a copyright brush

Magnetic Pen tool
Like the Pen tool, only easier

The Pen tool is one of the best ways to select an image, giving you the ability to save selections as paths, fill them with colour, create shape layers or adjust the selection using the various Path editing tools. Most people will reach for the Pen tool but if

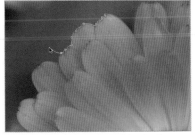

Let Photoshop help you out with selections

you choose the Freeform Pen tool instead, an interesting option appears in the top bar. This is a little checkbox called Magnetic. Click this box and the tool will cling to edges of images, so all you have to do is guide it around the area you want to select.

Quick duotone effect
Use Variations for instant edits

Photoshop ships with a very good Duotone command and if you are going to get your images printed professionally, this is the best method to use. However, if you like the look more than the science behind it, say a big hello to Variations.

Enjoy duotones in a fraction of the time

Open up a black and white image and then go to Image>Adjustments>Variations. Because the command works by adding or subtracting different hues, you essentially get a one-click duotone machine! Set it to Midtones and then click to get the effect you want.

Photoshop CS and above

WHITEN EYES
Improve portraits with ease

 Q I am in the midst of retouching some wedding photos for a friend but the eyes all look a bit dull and I want a way of making them sparkle. I'm having trouble getting a realistic effect.
Michael Hopkins

A We've already seen how Hue/Saturation can help calm down red skin. It can also help add realistic sparkle to eyes.

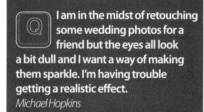

01 **Select the whites** Zoom into your image. Pick the tool of your choice and select the whites of one eye. Hold down Shift then select from the other. Go to Select>Feather and enter a Radius of 3.

02 **Reduce the colour** Go to Image>Adjustments>Hue/Saturation and then select a colour. Our image had pale yellow tints, so we picked Yellows. Drag the Saturation slider to the left.

03 **Now for light** You don't want dull eyes, so when you have removed the colour, set the Edit menu to Master and drag the Lightness slider to the right. Click OK and Cmd/Ctrl+D to deselect.

Easy montages

Q I've just got back from holiday and really want to create a scrapbook of the trip. Ideally I would like to create a montage but I am new to Photoshop and am more than a bit shaky with selections!
Josef Kovács

A Creating a montage is one of those things with a gazillion possible ways of doing it. Well maybe not a gazillion, but certainly more than a handful! Since you are just starting out, the easiest method is to use the Eraser tool. We shan't lie – it doesn't offer the smoothest result, but it does a pretty good job. Open up your scrapbook document and the photos you want to add. Drag each photo over to the scrapbook page to add them. Use the Move tool to position them where you want and Edit>Free Transform to alter the size (hold down Shift and click-drag a corner point to increase or decrease the size). For a smooth

Combine images quickly and easily with the Eraser tool

Soft focus effect
Go all romantic

Traditional photographers have to turn to a special filter if they want a soft focus effect, but us Photoshop peeps only need a Blur filter. Open your photo and duplicate it by pressing Cmd/Ctrl+J. Working on this duplicate layer, go to Filters>Blur>Gaussian Blur and start with a Radius of 12. Click OK and then head to the Opacity slider in the Layers palette and set this to 50% to bring some detail back. Experiment with the blur and opacity settings for your image.

Give your images a romantic feel with some soft focus

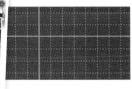

and effective scrapbook look, you need to make sure that the edges of different layers overlap each other. To do this, select the Eraser tool and choose a large, soft edge brush, set to 50% Opacity. Click a layer and then simply erase the edges. You will see the layer underneath appear where you have removed parts of the image. You can change the layer order by click-dragging one to where you want in the Layers palette.

High-contrast photo effects

I'm always looking for ways to make my portraits look different and really stand out, but have recently run up against a creative brick wall. Do you have any advice?
Ben Stockley

You don't say what skill level you are at, so we will play it safe with a simple but really effective technique. We will show how to give an image a high-contrast look, which is a favourite of editorial designers. Open your start image and duplicate it twice (you will then have three layers). Click the eye icon on the top layer, select the middle layer and desaturate it by going to Image>Adjustments>Desaturate. Lower the layer Opacity to 75-80% and then click the eye icon on the top layer to make it visible. With

Add some zing to portraits with this easy effect

this layer selected, go to the blending modes menu and pick Overlay to get the effect. You can calm it down using the Opacity slider, or try the Soft Light mode instead.

Reveal dark areas

I tend to leave my camera on Auto mode and have some landscape shots where the detail is hidden away in shadow. I've tried using Levels to fix this but the results don't look right. What can I do?
Jeff Jacobs

For this problem the best thing you can do is to pay a visit to the Image>Adjustments menu and

Shine light on areas that are hiding in the shadows

pick the Shadow/Highlight command. It will open up with Shadows set to 50% by default and, to be honest, just leaving it like this will fix the problem a lot of the time. If you need more help, though, drag the Shadows slider to the right to lighten the dark areas of your image using the preview to decide when you're happy. Click OK to commit to the edit.

> ## "The Shadow/Highlight command opens up with Shadows set to 50% by default… this will fix the problem a lot of the time"

Print with Picture Package
Get more prints for your buck

If you are printing from home, it makes sense to get as many prints on each sheet of paper as possible to help cut down on waste and expense. Photoshop has a nifty way of doing this called Picture Package. Found under File>Automate, it enables you to set the size of your paper and then choose from a series of layouts. You can apply it to just one image or a number. Once you have picked a layout, you can also edit it.

Let Photoshop arrange images for prints

Shine a spotlight
Focus attention with light effects

We are used to seeing spotlights on the stage pick out an object, but they are also useful for highlighting areas of an image. Photoshop has some preset spotlight settings found in Filters>Render>Lighting Effects that are very easy to use. Open up your image and then duplicate it. Now open the Lighting Effects filter and Flashlight from the Style menu. Use the side points around the circle to adjust the size and click OK. If the effect is too harsh, reduce the opacity of the spotlight layer.

Draw the viewer's eye using a spotlight

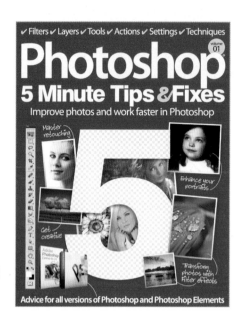

Learning Photo
We've got it cov

Order our copies of the very best creative bookazines and DVDs today

Photoshop CS5 Genius Guide
Over 200 pages of advice for Photoshop CS5 users, including tool guides, step-by-step workshops and video tutorials.
SRP: £12.99

Advanced Photoshop DVD vol 3
1,200 pages of professional Photoshop tutorials, interviews and features fully searchable and with free video tutorials.
SRP: £9.99

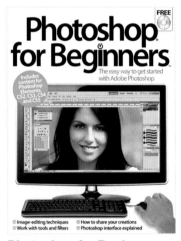

Photoshop for Beginners
This guide will walk you through everything you need to know about Photoshop. From Elements to CS5, you'll learn all the best ways to edit your images.
SRP: £12.99

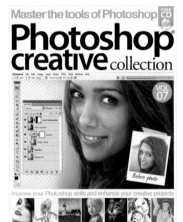

Photoshop Creative Collection vol 7
This latest addition to the Photoshop Collection includes excellent guides to help you become a Photoshop master.
SRP: £14.99

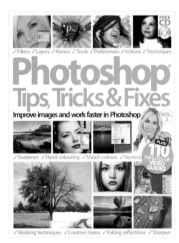

Photoshop Tips, Tricks & Fixes vol 2
The ultimate guide to Photoshop cheats. This fun guide will show you how to get the results you want from Photoshop fast!
SRP: £14.99

Professional Photoshop Book
Covering all the aspects of Adobe's suite, this is the perfect companion for anyone wishing to improve their digital creations.
SRP: £14.99

Beginner's Photoshop vol 3
This third volume covers over 50 new inspirational Photoshop projects in an easy-to-follow format complete with over an hour of video tutorials on the disc.
SRP: £12.99

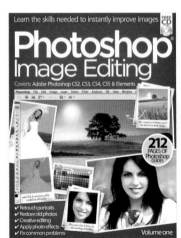

Photoshop Image Editing vol 1
Improve your photos with this guide to image-editing skills, from cloning and colour correction through to restoring old photos.
SRP: £12.99

shop?
ered